M000224267

OPERATION
BLUECOAT

THE BRITISH ARMOURED
BREAKOUT

Battleground Europe
NORMANDY

OPERATION BLUECOAT

THE BRITISH ARMOURED BREAKOUT

Ian Daglish

LEO COOPER

Published by
LEO COOPER
an imprint of
Pen & Sword Books Limited
47 Church Street, Barnsley, South Yorkshire S70 2AS
Copyright © Ian Daglish, 2003

ISBN 0 85052 912 3

A CIP catalogue of this book is available
from the British Library

Printed by CPI UK

For up-to-date information on other titles produced under the Leo Cooper
imprint, please telephone or write to:
Pen & Sword Books Ltd, FREEPOST SF5, 47 Church Street
Barnsley, South Yorkshire S70 2AS
Telephone 01226 734555

CONTENTS

Acknowledgements 6

Introduction 7

Chapter 1   MID JULY: SEEKING A BREAKOUT 9

Chapter 2   LATE JULY: THE BLUECOAT PLAN 21

Chapter 3   SUNDAY 30 JULY: CHURCHILLS AND JOCKS 29

Chapter 4   MONDAY 31 JULY: DICKIE'S BRIDGE 55

Chapter 5   TUESDAY 1 AUGUST: DAY OF BREAKTHROUGH 67

Chapter 6   WEDNESDAY 2 AUGUST: THRUST
             AND COUNTER THRUST 103

Chapter 7   THURSDAY 3 AUGUST: NO MAN'S LAND
             TO THE REAR 151

Chapter 8   FRIDAY 4 TO SUNDAY 6 AUGUST:
             THE LINE HOLDS 169

Chapter 9   AFTERMATH AND ASSESSMENT 179

             Notes for visitors 181

             TOUR 1 183

             TOUR 2 184

             TOUR 3 185

             Appendices I and II 187

             INDEX 189

ACKNOWLEDGEMENTS

No single source of information about events in 1944 can be relied upon totally. War diaries written during the action often reflect front line units' limited knowledge of the bigger picture, while old soldiers are sometimes the first to admit that memories fade after six decades. Some respected histories of the battles for Normandy perpetuate inaccuracies which have gained credence in the re-telling. However, by going back to original sources inaccuracies can often be exposed. Once a few pieces of the historical jigsaw are confirmed the rest of the puzzle can be solved using painstaking research and common sense. Visiting the battleground itself can often resolve doubts about the accuracy of accounts of the action.

Among the many to whom this author is grateful, special acknowledgment is extended to some who have made researching this book a particularly enjoyable experience. The helpful staff of the Public Records Office at Kew manage a national treasurehouse which is always a delight to explore. David Fletcher, Historian at The Tank Museum at Bovington, has tirelessly answered queries and sought out photographs. Yet another national treasure is the Air Photo Library at Keele University where Mrs M C Beech, Air Photo Archive Manager, has located images from the enormous collection in her custody. David Porter at the Tactical Doctrine Retrieval Cell has generously shared material formerly held at Staff College. The staff of Alderley Edge Library have triumphed in locating rare works needed by the author.

Personal insights have come from several former soldiers. Special thanks go to John Kenneth and Ron Lomas, 2/Argyll and Sutherland Highlanders; Charles Farrell, 3/(Tank) Scots Guards; and, for his constant encouragement, to Patrick Delaforce, 13/Royal Horse Artillery. Of the many individuals named in this narrative who are no longer with us, mention must go to Major J J How, 3/Monmouths, whose 1981 work *Normandy: The British Breakout* is highly recommended as a complementary account of Operation BLUECOAT.

The author is grateful to Her Majesty's Stationery Office for permission to use Crown Copyright material. Photographs on pages 35 and 38 are reproduced by kind permission of The Tank Museum. All aerial images are based on 1944 photo reconnaissance. Photographs taken by RAF aircraft operating out of Britain during the campaign have a particular poignancy and are © Crown Copyright 1944/MOD, reproduced with the permission of the Controller of Her Majesty's Stationery Office. Cover art is *Jagdpanther* by David Pentland.

INTRODUCTION

In August, 1815, the Duke of Wellington advised Sir Walter Scott against writing a history of the battle of Waterloo. 'The history of a battle is not unlike the history of a ball,' he wrote,

> 'Some individuals may recollect all the little events, of which the great result is the battle won or lost; but no individual can recollect the order in which, or the exact moment at which, they occurred, which makes all the difference as to their value or importance.'[1]

The Duke was writing of a battle fought just six weeks previously, involving fewer than a quarter of a million men; a battle fought over a single day, on a battlefield whose four corners were visible to the naked eye. Operation BLUECOAT took place six decades ago, involved far greater numbers than Waterloo, and in a week of fighting spread over a battlefield of more than 300 square kilometres. If we accept the Duke's point of view, how ever can the story of BLUECOAT be told?

Of course, Wellington's regiments did not keep signal logs, nor did each have an Intelligence Officer charged with recording the day's events with entries in the unit War Diary. (Even in the meticulously-kept logbooks of Nelson's Royal Navy, an event as specific as the opening shots of the battle of Trafalgar was recorded by different British ships at a variety of times spanning sixty-eight minutes[2]!) Virtually every regiment engaged in BLUECOAT has left at least one official history and often a number of unofficial ones. The modern historian has access to numerous personal memoirs and invaluable details such as aerial photographs of the battlefield.

But Wellington had a point. An account covering every detail of every action fought by every unit involved in Operation BLUECOAT would fill many volumes. This book is less ambitious. While presenting an overview of the battle, it focuses on certain episodes selected for their importance to the outcome. These include examples of virtually every type of 1944 armoured combat: from infantry tanks to specialized flame-throwing and mine-sweeping tanks; from lightly armoured reconnaissance units to the heaviest battle tanks of the Second World War. And of course the vital interactions between armour and infantry. The experiences of both sides, German as well as Allied, are presented, often separately in order to show how little each side knew of the others progress in a swirling mêlée under the hot summer sun between Caumont and Vire.

Notes on terminology

1. Original documents are quoted as accurately as possible – in some cases with non-standard spelling or punctuation, or military abbreviations such as British Army 'tk' for tank, 'fmn' for formation and German 'Pz.Gr.' for 'Panzer Grenadier'.

2. German unit titles and ranks are generally given in the German style. Also, German references to gun calibres are given in centimetres, vs. Allied guns in inches or millimetres.

3. Hill spot heights are given in metres as on 1944 maps, which sometimes do not correspond exactly to modern trigonometry. They are of course close to the altitudes marked on modern French maps, but with so many hills having similar spot heights, confusion can arise. Therefore, the first time each spot height is mentioned, its equivalent on modern maps is shown in brackets. A similar procedure is used for French road numbers, as these nowadays rarely retain their 1944 designations.

4. Many French place names were recorded in 1944 with a variety of spellings. For consistency and to aid the modern visitor, place names are shown as they appear on modern French maps.

References

1 *Men of Waterloo*, John Sutherland, 1966, p xiii.
2 *Trafalgar*, John Terraine, 1975 ISBN 0-88405-387-3, p 204-205.

Chapter One

Mid July –
SEEKING A BREAKOUT

STAGNATION AND CRITICISM

By the end of July, Allied forces had been fighting in Normandy for seven long weeks. After the initial achievement of securing a foothold on Hitler's Fortress Europe, progress had been slow. At least the Americans could be seen to have secured most of the Cotentin peninsula, and could offset their casualties against territorial gains that made good news headlines. But on the British side euphoria turned to frustration as it became apparent that the front had (in Field Marshal Bernard Law Montgomery's own words) 'glued up'. British losses mounted and success seemed to come no closer.

For Montgomery's many enemies among the Allies, it was easy to point

Montgomery strides confidently across the beach in Normandy.

to 'phase lines' not achieved, and to Germans deftly blocking each British attempt to break out of the Normandy bridgehead. The Americans could claim the seizure of Cherbourg, against which the city of Caen (supposed to have fallen to the British on D-Day itself) was still untaken a month later. The front line moved over Caen only slowly, painfully, and ingloriously. Its ruins and stunned surviving inhabitants finally fell into Allied hands on 10 July, only a week before American forces could trumpet their seizure of the strategically important city of Saint Lô.

As far as personal publicity went, the austere Montgomery could not compete with the newly arrived American Lieutenant General George S Patton as good news copy. Patton's 'secret' arrival in Normandy on 6 July quickly became a news media event, eagerly attended even on a 'no notes, no quotes' basis, during which he reportedly stated that a breakout from the beachhead was unlikely 'with that

9

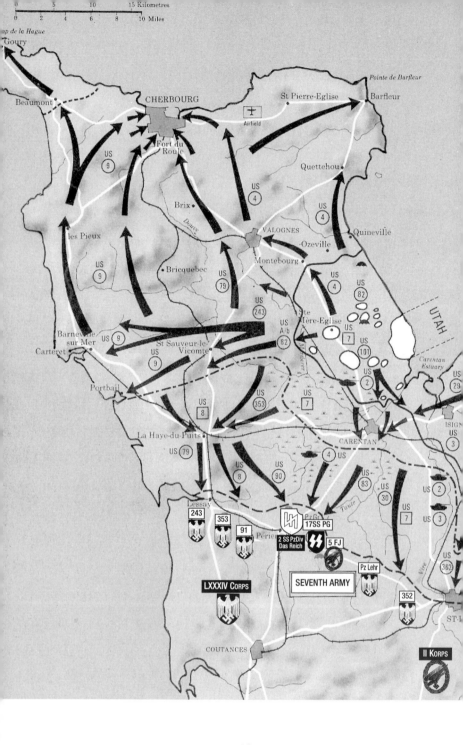

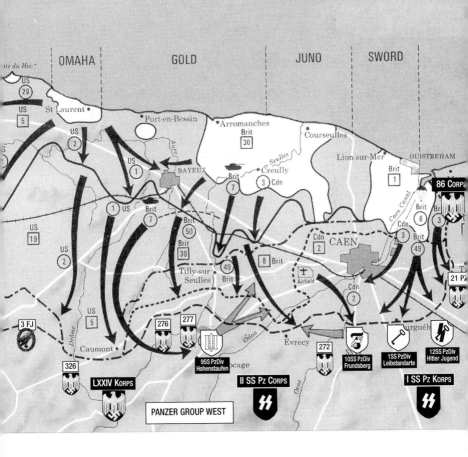

Territory gained by the Allies after six weeks – D-Day to 25 July 1944

Held by Allies at 2400 hrs on D-Day
Front line 10 June
Front line 17 June
Front line 30 June
Front line 24 July
Allied attacks
German counter-attacks
Division
Corps
Allied Armoured Division
Allied Airborne Division

Baie de la Seine

OMAHA GOLD JUNO SWORD

US 29
US 5
St Laurent
US 2
Pointe du Hoc
US 1
Port-en-Bessin
Arromanches
Brit 30
Courseulles
Lion-sur-Mer
OUISTREHAM
BAYEUX
Creully
Brit 7
3 Cdn
Aure
Seulles
Brit 1
86 Corps
1 US
Brit 7
Brit 50
Brit 30
Brit 6
Brit 3
CAEN
Cdn 3
Brit 49
US 19
US 2
Tilly-sur-Seulles
Brit 49
Cdn 2
8 Brit
Airfield
Cdn 2
21 Pz
Caen Canal
US 5
3 FJ
276 277
Odon
Evrecy
272
10SS PzDiv Frundsberg
1SS PzDiv Leibstandarte
12SS PzDiv Hitler Jugend
Caumont
Bocage
Drôme
Orne
326
LXXIV Korps
II SS Pz Corps
I SS Pz Korps
PANZER GROUP WEST

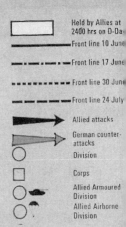

11

British stretcher-bearers pick their way through the ruined streets of Caen, smashed by Allied bombing.

Americans move into St Lô. The American forces were making progress whilst the British were involved in heavy fighting around Caen and making little progress.

little fart in charge'.[1] No one doubted whom he meant. And while the quote was – for the time being – unattributable, American newspapers were already questioning whether America's British allies were really pulling their weight.

When Field Marshal Montgomery came to write his memoirs, he laid great emphasis on a problem new to commanders in 1944 but all too familiar today. Over half of the 'Introduction' to Montgomery's own history of the campaign in

The newly-arrived Patton with Montgomery. Their mutual dislike is hidden in front of General Bradley.

north west Europe is devoted to the conflict of interest between military security and the need of 'the Press' to find news stories every day of the week.[2] This conflict put increasing pressure on the British commander of ground forces as the Normandy campaign dragged on, and it is no small tribute to Montgomery that his outward optimism and drive endured in the face of mounting criticism.

THE DEFENDERS

It is a truism of warfare that your enemy's position always looks better to you than it does to him. The defenders of Normandy were suffering extremely. At the end of June, Operation EPSOM was launched against the élite *12 SS-Panzer Division 'Hitlerjugend'*, holding the line of the Odon River, south west of Caen. The Hitler Youth division resisted tenaciously but could not withstand the hammer blow of a corps-level assault backed by an opening bombardment of nine hundred guns. Within days, the fight had sucked in the newly arriving *II Panzer Korps*. Both its *9 and 10 SS Panzer Divisions* had been flung into the front line literally piecemeal, as

Youngsters in the SS, in the fighting in the Normandy battles they proved to be formidable adversaries.

their component battalions struggled to complete their long journey from the Ukraine. Instead of leading an armoured drive back to the beaches, these units were drawn onto the killing fields of the Royal Artillery, then stopped by relatively inexperienced British infantry. Within days of its arrival, *II Panzer Korps* experienced losses in weapons, vehicles and combat veterans which blunted the offensive capability of the strongest armoured formation in Normandy.[3]

EISENHOWER AND MONTGOMERY

As the second month of the Battle of Normandy unfolded, British casualties grew to levels far exceeding the British campaign plan. Losses of infantry alone up to 9 August came to 34,000, against the prediction of 25,000. Criticism of the Commander likewise grew. In mid-July, the apparent strategic failure of Operation GOODWOOD led to further questions concerning Montgomery's competence, not least from a Royal Air Force resentful of calls for heavy ground support which was seen as distracting the bombers from their primary role of prosecuting the strategic bombing offensive against Germany.[4]

Eisenhower, as Supreme Commander, had the unenviable job of keeping the peace between his squabbling generals.

Montgomery's boss, Supreme Commander Dwight D Eisenhower, made clear his own doubts. As early as 12 June, Eisenhower visited Normandy in a mood reported as 'buoyant and inspired'. But by the end of the visit he was highly critical of Montgomery's failure to make progress, prompting talk of timidity and possible sackings. On 7 July, the day after another acrimonious meeting, he wrote to Montgomery, 'We must use all possible energy in a determined effort to prevent a stalemate'[5]. Characteristically, Montgomery refused to be deflected by such criticism.

In spite of his critics, and regardless of real setbacks, Montgomery stuck to his overall plan. At the tactical level, he ensured that the Germans' undeniable superiority in weapons and battle tactics were as far as possible negated by his own forces' superiority in logistics, artillery and air

14

power. At the operational level, he succeeded in wresting the initiative away from the German Army in Normandy. And, perhaps most importantly, at the strategic level he demonstrably achieved his aim of tying down the Panzer divisions in defensive positions.

The essential fact remains: throughout the campaign for Normandy, the German army was kept on the defensive, its best units suffering continual attrition, and its *matériel* inexorably running down at a time when the Allies had parks of tanks ready and waiting in England. General Montgomery remained outwardly confident. He stuck doggedly to his strategy of hitting the enemy with alternating hammer blows ('colossal cracks', as he liked to call them).[6] No sooner did Operation GOODWOOD terminate than yet another bloody battering commenced, this time with Operation SPRING as the Canadians bludgeoned their way around the south west of Caen. By the last week of July, Montgomery was holding seven Panzer divisions in front of the British sector, as opposed to two in front of the Americans.

THE COBRA PLAN

Like the British, the Americans had underestimated the effect of the Normandy countryside on the campaign they were about to fight. The close bocage with its dense hedgerows was ideal defensive terrain. American armoured units which had been worked-up for invasion on the wide open spaces of Dartmoor were unprepared for such country. Progress was also hampered by the US Army's lack of a tank gun capable of taking on heavy German armour. British armoured regiments at least had one

The Firefly, with its 17-pounder gun, gave the British an even chance against the panzers.

17-pounder armed Firefly in each troop of four Sherman tanks. 'At last', desert veterans felt, 'a gun which one could trust to get its teeth really deep into any German tank it met'. The Americans had none. American doctrine still viewed the Sherman tank as a weapon of exploitation. Its low-velocity 75mm gun was intended not for tank-vs.-tank combat but for exploiting gaps in the enemy line, 'the proper use of armor' according to General Patton.[7]

The Sherman tank, designed with mobile warfare in mind.

Supply of artillery ammunition remained a concern to the Americans throughout the campaign, with rationing being imposed on units which normally expected to back any offensive action with ample artillery support. Losses of equipment – rifles, mortars, machine guns – were higher than expected but could quickly be made up

American artillery men arm 105mm howitzer shells.

(from what the US Army's official history describes as 'unnecessarily high quantities' of reserves).[8] Less easily rectified were unexpectedly high losses of infantry, particularly riflemen. American planners predicted that the infantry would account for seventy per cent of combat losses in Normandy. This proved an underestimate. The actual percentage accounted for by the American infantry in June and July was eighty-five, and most of these were the battle-hardened front-line riflemen.

In summary: the depth of the American beachhead in Normandy was not much greater in mid-July than it had been in mid-June. The US Army was confident of its ability – honed in Tunisia – to use mobility and firepower to outrun German forces in a war of movement. But instead of the mobile campaign planned, there were growing fears that stagnation was setting in, in a manner reminiscent of the First World War. The American front too was 'gluing up'.

Something was needed to break the deadlock. Both seaborne and airborne outflanking operations were seriously considered. But, contrary to German apprehensions, few troops trained in amphibious assault remained in England. As for airborne operations, the two American airborne divisions dropped on 6 June had stayed in the line longer than planned before being extracted back to England, and the need to divert 400 transport aircraft in support of the landings in southern France ruled out any substantial drop. Many of the élite units of the British 6th Airborne Division were left serving as front line infantry until attrition left insufficient of them to repeat the successes of 6 June. One wonders what

American infantry follow up the tanks.

American troops examine a Panther tank of *Panzer Lehr Division* knocked out by carpet bombing. Mangled MkIVs below.

Air Marshal Leigh-Mallory discusses the situation in France with aircrew of Ninth Air Force.

John Howard's 2/ Oxf and Bucks, whose six gliders took Pegasus Bridge, could have achieved had they been preserved to attempt a *coup de main* against Arnhem bridge in September, 1944![9]

The Americans' chosen solution was carpet bombing. Operation COBRA would begin with a massive aerial bombardment by strategic as well as tactical air forces. As the final details were worked out during the second week of July, American hopes turned to real optimism: once cracked open, the German front might shatter, permitting exploitation as far as the ports of Brittany.

The British were broadly supportive of the COBRA plan. Montgomery (still in command of all ground forces) approved it on 18 July. Air Chief Marshal Leigh-Mallory, usually resistant to any interruption of the strategic bombing of Germany, went so far as to express disappointment that the RAF was not invited to take part (though he accepted the argument that over-cratering was to be avoided, and that American air power would suffice).[10]

COBRA began inauspiciously. On the afternoon of 24 July, in bad visibility and as frantic efforts were made to recall the bombers, 685 tons of high explosive and fragmentation munitions were nevertheless dropped through the haze. In spite of elaborate precautions, American 'friendly fire' losses were incurred and recriminations flew. The day's operations were called off.

American breakout during Operation COBRA.

Nevertheless, COBRA was reinstated and the following day over 4,000 tons of bombs fell on less than ten square miles. American casualties were again suffered, but whole German units including the élite *Panzer Lehr Division* were obliterated.[11] An American breakthrough commenced which, once the crust of German resistance was broken, would lead to Avranches and beyond.

References

1 *Death of a Nazi Army*, William B Breuer, 1985, ISBN 0-8128-8520-1; *A Soldier's Story*, Omar N Bradley, 1951, p 355-356.
2 *Normandy to the Baltic*, Field Marshal The Viscount Montgomery of Alamein, 1946, p xii-xiii.
3 *Im Feuersturm Letzter Kriegsjahre*, Wilhelm Tieke, 1975, ISBN 3-921242-18-5, p 148-198.
4 *Against Odds: Reflections on the British Army, 1914-1945*, Dominick Graham, 1999, ISBN 0-333-66858-8, p 184-186.
5 *US Army in World War Two: Breakout and Pursuit*, Martin Blumenson, 1961, Library of Congress Catalog Card 61-6000, p 119.
6 *Montgomery and 'Colossal Cracks', The 21st Army Group in Northwest Europe, 1944-45*, Stephen Ashley Hart, 2001, ISBN 0-275-96162-1.
7 General George S Patton, March, 1945.
8 Blumenson, p 179.
9 Blumenson, p 185-187; *Pegasus Bridge*, Stephen E Ambrose, 1984, ISBN 0-671-71261-6, p 156-157.
10 Bradley, p 341.
11 *La Panzer Lehr Division*, Jean-Claude Perrigault, 1995, ISBN 2-84048-081-6, p 274-280.

CHAPTER TWO

Late July –
THE BLUECOAT PLAN

THE FORERUNNERS OF 'BLUECOAT'

On 10 July, Montgomery held a conference at which General Bradley (US First Army) freely admitted his concerns at lack of progress, and referred to the COBRA plan which was about to be prepared. Montgomery was supportive, assuring the Americans that he would continue to hold the Panzer divisions on the British front. Lieutenant General Miles Dempsey (commanding British Second Army) went further, initiating planning for a new British offensive at the extreme eastern end of the bridgehead, to ensure the German defenders were kept off-balance. Initially cool on the idea, Montgomery nevertheless grew increasingly keen on executing a British breakout simultaneous with the Americans.

As early as mid-June, Operation DREADNOUGHT had proposed advancing around the east side of Caen, but had been dismissed. Since D-Day, bitter fighting had continued throughout this area, but the bridgehead on the right bank of the Orne River remained shallow. The British viewed this avenue of attack as just too narrow. The few Orne River

General Miles Dempsey with Eisenhower.

bridges seemed too great a logistic bottleneck for any offensive east of the river to promise satisfactory results. Now, in search of a plan to draw German attention to the extreme eastern flank of the Normandy battle, these plans were reviewed, and the result was Operation GOODWOOD.

OPERATION GOODWOOD

Commencing on 18 July, Operation GOODWOOD launched three armoured divisions southwards down a narrow corridor in the general direction of Falaise. After two days, Montgomery closed down the battle, having gained thirty-four square miles of territory for the loss of 500 tanks and over 4,000 men. Montgomery expressed satisfaction at the outcome. Eisenhower was furious. He had expected a major breakthrough and felt let down. Once again, talk of sackings was in the air. Air Chief Marshal Sir Arthur Tedder urged Eisenhower to get rid of Montgomery or risk 'your own people thinking you have sold them out to the British'.[1] Flying to Normandy on 20 July, in weather that grounded all other aircraft that morning, Eisenhower bluntly told Montgomery that he lacked vigour and drive. The following day he wrote asking whether the two of them 'see eye to eye on the big problems'[2] and pointedly reminded the ground forces

Montgomery at his headquarters flanked by Eisenhower and Air Chief Marshal Tedder. Smiles for the camera but Tedder was urging Eisenhower to sack the British commander.

commander that a time was coming when American forces in the theatre would outnumber British, leading to the reactivation of First US Army Group under a separate, American, commander.

Montgomery remained – outwardly at least – unmoved by criticism. Far from bowing to his superior's wishes, it seems likely Monty conceived his next offensive as a straightforward continuation of his strategy of alternating hammer blows on different parts of the front. The inspiration for Operation BLUECOAT appears to have come from Montgomery's loyal supporter, Lieutenant General Dempsey. But the plan fitted Montgomery's own strategy perfectly. GOODWOOD had drawn German units onto the British front south east of Caen; it had chewed up the defending formations, and several newcomers would have to remain to hold the line. So, the British would strike somewhere else.

THE BLUECOAT PLAN

BLUECOAT was based on the simple observation that the British right flank, the boundary with the US First Army, was opposed by only weak enemy forces. ULTRA decrypts during the last week of July confirmed to Montgomery that German forces were still massing around Caen, still fearful of a resumption of the GOODWOOD offensive in the direction of Falaise.

BLUECOAT gives an interesting example of how successfully ULTRA could be used in support of operational planning. As Montgomery finalized his orders for BLUECOAT, ULTRA revealed that the *21 Panzerdivision* was being pulled out of the line around Caen.[3] Montgomery deduced that this unit was being sent westward even *before* von Kluge had decided to do exactly that. So, in this case, ULTRA signalled a German decision that had not yet been made at the time of the decrypt. Little wonder that Hitler fumed at his enemies' apparent ability to penetrate his deepest secrets: 'How does the enemy learn our thoughts from us?'[4] But since the bomb plot of 20 July, Hitler saw traitors everywhere. It was easier for him to blame dissidents within his own signals services than to credit the possibility of the Enigma machines' transmissions being regularly decoded by brilliant minds gathered at Bletchley Park.

Having done all he could to 'fix' his enemy in the east, Montgomery ordered the move of Dempsey's Second Army to the far west of the British line.

XXX CORPS

XXX Corps under Lieutenant General Bucknall would lead the attack. Comprising 43rd (Wessex), 50th (Northumbrian), and 7th Armoured Divisions, XXX Corps expected to face only a single, depleted German *276 Infanterie Division*.

Lieutenant General Bucknall, commander of XXX Corps.

On the face of it, this was a very powerful Corps. The 43rd Division – the 'Wessex Wyverns' – had undergone some shattering experiences in the fighting in the Odon valley and on Hill 112 [modern 112]. Its fiery General Thomas had gained notoriety along with a reputation for 'pressing on' regardless of losses. 50th Northumbrian had suffered similarly, landing on D-Day and in action so frequently that it experienced severe officer losses and a generally high level of fatigue. This gave rise to complaints that 'Fling 'em in Monty' was working the division too hard.[5] The division was tired.

Finally, 7th Armoured Division was under a cloud. The heroes of the desert war had found their past experience gained in the open spaces of Libya and Tunisia did not prepare them for the close bocage country. Here an infantryman with a *Panzerfaust* could be lurking behind every bush, and a well positioned antitank gun could quickly devastate a whole troop of advancing tanks. 7th Armoured had swung overnight from recklessness to over-caution. Dempsey's view of the division's performance at Villers-Bocage in mid-June was:

'...by this time, 7th Armoured Division was living on its reputation and the whole handling of that battle was a disgrace.'[6]

A gunner attached to the division gave a more sympathetic assessment.

'The chaps who had been in the desert detested Normandy... you could not see a thing half the time... In the desert, we could see them but not knock them out; in Europe we could knock them out but not see them.'

The division's late arrival and lack of apparent commitment during the GOODWOOD battle led to further questions being asked. The commander of 11th Armoured Division complained:

'I may say 7th Armoured Division did not put in an appearance before 5 p.m. ... I cursed both my old division and my old brigade!'[7]

Operation BLUECOAT was to add little to the 7th Armoured Division's reputation.

A concealed SS *Panzergrenadier* armed with a *Panzerfaust*, lies in wait for Allied tanks.

VIII CORPS

Covering XXX Corps' right flank, on the boundary with the American First Army, and facing the 326. *Infanteriedivision* would be Lieutenant General Sir Richard O'Connor's VIII Corps. For the only time in its history, VIII Corps was going into battle with all the units that had been present at its formation and through pre-invasion training. O'Connor later maintained that BLUECOAT was the Corps' finest battle.

Major General O'Connor, commander of VIII Corps, with Montgomery.

The one infantry division, 15th Scottish, had acquitted itself well in its introduction to combat during Operation EPSOM at the end of June. It had gained further experience since then in the hard fighting around the Odon River valley and Hill 113 [modern 114].[8] In theory, the division was tired and due for a rest on the right flank of the forthcoming operation.

In fact, most of the regiments in the division had emerged from the fighting around the Odon with their morale intact and regimental traditions enhanced. Reinforcements were absorbed and equipment replaced. Many men were able to enjoy brief periods of rest. Ron Lomas of 2/Argyll and Sutherland Highlanders recalls his forty-eight hours leave at St-Aubin-sur-Mer, spent in 'extra-wide luxurious slit trenches.' But the narrow beachhead did not allow a complete escape from the war: 'The Germans bombed every night, the guns fired. Some rest!' Fortunately for Ron, he teamed up with two civilians from the merchant navy who took him out to their ship where he enjoyed a meal, a bunk, and breakfast before being returned to the beach to find his mates already gone – to join the regiment at Caumont.

Assigned to support of 15th Scottish was 6th Guards Tank Brigade with its three battalions of Churchill infantry tanks. These old friends had practised tank-infantry co-operation with the Scots before the invasion, but the tanks had not reached Normandy in time for EPSOM.

The two armoured divisions of XXX Corps were 11th (the 'Black Bull') and Guards Armoured. Together, these represented a formidable concentration of force, although under different styles of management. Montgomery had severe doubts about the leadership of Guards Armoured

Division. As early as February he had asked Dempsey to sack the division's commander, Major General Adair, which Dempsey was happy to do. Adair was spared only by O'Connor's refusal to concoct an unfavourable report on the general's performance, and quite probably also by a shortage of replacement candidates who would be considered acceptable by the Guards.[9]

By contrast, 11th Armoured Division's Major General 'Pip' Roberts was a rising star. Aged thirty seven, he was the youngest British divisional commander. He was experienced: no British general had spent longer fighting in the turret of a tank. And he was confident: denied permission to sack a particular senior officer, Roberts had gone over the heads of O'Connor and Dempsey to receive permission directly from Montgomery.[10] 'Pip' Roberts was a desert fighter who was nevertheless able to learn the different tactics needed to succeed in Normandy. Dempsey had assigned VIII Corps a supporting role in the

Major General 'Pip' Roberts commanding 11th Armoured Division

knowledge that some of its units had taken a battering, in particular 11th Armoured which had lost 191 tanks at GOODWOOD a fortnight before. But the performance of VIII Corps was to exceed expectations. Like the 15th Scottish, 11th Armoured Division was replenished, reorganised, and far from downhearted. 'Pip' Roberts freely admitted that 'It was not until our third battle in Normandy that we got it right'.[11] Now, after EPSOM and GOODWOOD, he was ready to show what 11th Armoured could achieve.

IMPLEMENTING BLUECOAT

Two of 15th Scottish Division's three brigades had been moved west to the Caumont area as early as 23 July, to relieve the American 5th Division before the start of COBRA. Relieving an American unit was a novel experience, and a welcome one, as the Americans were well supplied and to the great delight of the Jocks 'not particular about what they left behind'. To Robert Woollcombe, an officer of 6/King's Own Scottish Borderers:

> *'Hitherto the Americans were a kind of legend beyond the horizon, but here they were, very decidedly, with hearts as big as houses. They seemed thrilled to see us, and proudly showed their automatic rifles to groups of admiring Jocks.'[12]*

Corporal Ron Lomas of 2/Argyll and Sutherland Highlanders recalls equipment, weapons, and even boxes of cigarettes left lying about:

> *'I gathered up hundreds of cigarettes, and found a marvellous officer's*

coat just hanging on the branch of a tree; I was not allowed to wear it though, and in the end I gave it to an American officer for just 200 cigarettes.'

An American position abandoned during the Normandy campaign and littered with supplies and items of equipment. A virtual treasure trove for their Allies and locals.

The Scots settled into their new quarters, little troubled by the distant Germans of *326. Division* who had themselves only recently been moved to this quiet part of the line. Although some aggressive patrolling was organised in search of prisoners for interrogation, little contact was made with the enemy who were content to stay well back from the front. The sector was quiet, and it made a pleasant change to be in an area where houses were largely undamaged and farmers worked peacefully in the fields. The Jocks were also pleased to have access to a glut of dairy products which the locals were no longer able to send to the Paris markets.

For other units of Dempsey's Second Army the move was less easy. Most units did not receive movement orders until late on 28 July. 43rd Infantry Division was just three days into a rest period after their gruelling ordeal on Hill 112, and the return to action was unlooked for. At least the infantry had a reasonably short journey across the British sector. They marched through areas between Bayeux and Caumont little damaged by fighting, thanks to 50th Division's rapid advance inland during June. Progress was harder for the armoured divisions, whose routes took them across the supply lines of both XII and XXX Corps, and hardest of all was the journey of Guards Armoured Division, starting from the far bank of the Orne River. Moving forward to their first encounter with the enemy, 6th Guards Armoured Brigade's Churchill tanks were given 'little time for reconnaissance or very detailed planning'. Their night drive wound to and fro through orchards, sunken lanes and narrow tracks, and the first job on the morning of 29 July was to send out search parties to locate and bring in missing vehicles. 'Pip' Roberts of 11th Armoured Division recalled:

> *'Corps orders arrived at our HQ during the cross-country march, so that our orders to brigades arrived at around 02.00 on 30 July and 'H' hour for the attack was 06.55 hours. It was a scramble, but just worked.'*[13]

References

1 *Overlord: D-Day and the Battle for Normandy*, Max Hastings, 1984, ISBN 0-330-28691-9, P 281; Graham, p 186.
2 Blumenson, p 195.
3 *Ultra in the West: The Normandy Campaign of 1944 -45*, Ralph Bennett, 1979, ISBN 0-09-139330-2, p 108-111.
4 Bennett, p 114.
5 *Against Odds*, Dominick Graham, 1999, ISBN 0-333-66858-8, p 165.
6 Graham, p 167.
7 *From the Desert to the Baltic*, Major General G P B Roberts, 1987, ISBN 0-7183-0639-2, p 177.
8 *The History of the Fifteenth Scottish Division*, Lieutenant General H G Martin, 1948, p 29-79.
9 *Military Training in the British Army 1940-44 From Dunkirk to D-Day*, Timothy Harrison Place, 2000, ISBN, 0-7146-5037-4, p 126; Ashley Hart, p 142.
10 Roberts, p 164-165.
11 Roberts, p 159.
12 *Lion Rampant*, Robert Woolcombe, 1955, p 102.
13 Roberts, p 185.

Chapter Three

Sunday 30 July –
CHURCHILLS AND JOCKS

THE VIII CORPS BREAK-IN

The BLUECOAT role assigned to XXX Corps was to punch a hole through the German front line towards Cahagnes and then on to Point 361 [modern 358], a feature on the eastern side of the dominating Bois du Homme ridge. Meanwhile, VIII Corps was to protect XXX Corps' right from the risk of flank attack, while also exploiting any opportunities for an armoured breakthrough that might arise.

With 11th Armoured Division ordered to set off south west towards Dampierre, 15th Scottish with 6th Guards Tanks 'under command' was to move due south to take Point 309 [modern 308], a conical hill between the small town of St-Martin-des-Besaces to the west and the thickly wooded massif of the Bois du Homme to the east. Sometimes referred to as 'Quarry Hill', this feature not only dominated the main road south, through St-Martin-des-Besaces, but also was an important observation point, from which the departing Americans claimed to have suffered occasional harassing fire. Strategically, Hill 309, the smaller Hill 226 known as Le Homme, and the wooded massif of the Bois du Homme formed an important anchor for the defence of the whole region. This was certainly the German view. General Straube of *LXXIV Korps* had said of Hill 309:

'It is the key... It must not be allowed to fall into enemy hands.'

Regarding the attachment of 6th Guards Tank Brigade to the 15th Scottish, it should be noted that in the British Army of 1944, commanders of armoured units frequently dreaded being placed 'under command' of infantry formations. British infantry generals, including Montgomery himself, often failed to appreciate the strengths and weaknesses of armour. As one unit history put it:

'This was the horror of belonging to an independent armoured brigade; one changed hands from day to day like a library book. The Regiment would be flung into battle at a moment's notice with infantry who had never had experience of co-operating with tanks.'[1]

Some disastrous failures in Normandy resulted from lack of mutual support. In the case of 6th Guards Brigade, there was an excellent understanding with the infantry of 15th Scottish. Infantry companies and tank troops had worked closely together in England; individual officers knew one another; bonds of trust had been formed. For reasons of his own, Montgomery then substituted 6th Guards with 31st Tank Brigade, with the result that the first actions of 15th Scottish Division were not well integrated with the infantry tanks. Only in mid-July did 6th Guards Tanks cross to Normandy to rejoin VIII Corps just in time for BLUECOAT.[2] On 29 July, the newly reunited 15th and Guardsmen came to last-minute agreements on tactics. As the Scots' divisional history recalled:

> *'What with "O" Groups, joint tank and infantry reconnaissances and other preparations, 29th July was a strenuous day.'*[3]

Corps – and division – frontages were narrow. The ground to be covered was some of the densest bocage in Normandy, and the axis of attack ran directly across some dramatic ridge lines. This was the 'Suisse Normande', the little Switzerland in Normandy, defensive terrain where even depleted and tired German defenders might sell ground dearly. Correspondingly, 15th Scottish Major General MacMillan planned a narrow-fronted, multi-phased attack, with just two of his nine infantry battalions in the first wave.

FORMING UP

The initial breakthrough was to be led by 227 Brigade, strengthened by 9/Cameronians for a total of four battalions. In the first phase, just two battalions were to lead the way. Moving down off the Caumont ridge, 9/Cameronians on the right would secure the hamlet of Sept Vents, while on the left 2/Gordon Highlanders would clear the Lutain Wood, both battalions supported by 4/Tank Grenadier Guards, with troops of Sherman 'Crab' mine-clearing flail tanks and Churchill 'Crocodile' flame-throwing tanks on call.

Each infantry battalion advanced on a two-company front. One of the lessons learned in Normandy had been the sheer difficulty of locating the enemy, and the need for the infantry to minimize troops leading the way and maximize those held in reserve for manoeuvre when the enemy was located. One colonel (in 43rd Division) recalled:

> *'The opening bid in a battalion attack would be one company forward with another in immediate support as moppers up. The rest of the men would be held in reserve. These tactics were based on the fact that in the battalion, at company and platoon level, one seldom knew with any reasonable degree of accuracy the enemy's exact position. Great depth and the maximum volume of firepower was emphasised for all types of attack.'*[4]

British infantry advancing over open ground.

On the morning of 30 July, we can envisage each of the two objectives being approached by a wave of about two hundred riflemen, strung out across half a kilometre. Small groups of seven or eight men advanced at walking pace, well separated, across thickly-hedged fields varying from 100 metres across down to 50 metres or less. Unlike their German counterparts, the groups advanced more or less in unison. This was largely to ensure that their progress was closely synchronised with the development of the broader battle, with its complex orchestration of infantry, tanks, artillery, and air power. To each company of roughly one hundred men was assigned a troop of three Churchill infantry tanks loosely in support, though the ability of the tanks to follow the infantry closely was severely limited by the terrain. On the day, the tanks had to follow as best they could using the few narrow lanes and any serviceable breaches they could find in the hedgerows. The leading Churchills pressed forward, often out of sight of their fellow tanks, sometimes even out of radio communication as aerials were torn off. Individual commanders in this first wave supported any infantry they came across, or who sought them out.

Formed up before dawn, the first wave of infantry stepped off over the Caumont ridge at 06.55 hours. Under a leaden overcast and shrouded by the early morning mist, they passed through the outpost lines of 10/HLI and on down the forward slopes into the valley. There was no preliminary artillery bombardment, the first guns firing only as the infantry advanced, though since 06.15 hours fighter-bomber aircraft had been engaging enemy

Vehicles of various types await their turn to move up.

positions ahead. As the leading infantry companies departed, their places were immediately taken by men of the follow-up units, while vehicles crammed into every lane and three-deep behind every hedgerow awaited their turn to move out. Following the fighter-bombers came yet more air support as 1,300 medium and heavy bombers began to pound the landscape ahead. Their approach was masked by the overcast, but after releasing their bombs they turned north for home. The British troops were in turn impressed by the thunder of the bombs, reassured by the continuing throb of the engines, and thrilled when four-engined Lancaster bombers northbound on their way home to England roared over their heads.

SEPT VENTS AND LUTAIN WOOD

The enemy response was quick in coming. Within ten minutes of stepping off, both advancing battalions were taking losses from enemy artillery and mortar fire. Gordons and Cameronians alike lost company commanders in the opening salvoes. Some confusion resulted. The Cameronians' D Company commander was lost on the Start Line, and the only other officer present was a newly-arrived reinforcement.[5] The company's advance stalled until the commander of A Company, himself out of radio contact with battalion headquarters, took over. Further men were lost to unmarked antipersonnel mines, many laid by the Americans, while German antitank mines were also found, and the infantry regiments'

Lutain
Wood

3/Sqn Grenadier Guards

2/Gordon Highlanders

Caumont

2 Sqn Gren Grds

9/Cameronians

1 Sqn Gren Grds

le Vieux Bourg

Sunken Lane (p34)

Sept Vents

Sunken Lane (p34)

N

0   500m

Churchill tanks form up in the high Normandy grain alongside the infantry they are to support.

organic pioneer platoons were overwhelmed by the task of clearing them.

Behind the infantry the first of the supporting Grenadier Guards Churchill tanks crested the ridge, two squadrons, each of up to eighteen gun tanks, making for Sept Vents and a third squadron for the Lutain Wood. By this time, smoke from the aerial bombardment filled the valley and visibility forward was virtually nil. Tank commanders straining for a view outside their turrets were picked off by snipers or felled by shards of mortar bombs. In such close country, the tanks' movement was predictable and the antitank mines had been artfully sited.

On the right flank, the Grenadiers' 1 Squadron of Churchills struggled

The sunken lane north of Sept Vents. This had been sown with mines. Immobilised tanks had to be hauled out of the way to make room for the flail tank to clear the way. (See map on page 33)

A Sherman 'Crab' flail tank in Normandy. Note the station-keeping signals for following tanks, above the large panier for dispensing chalk dust to mark the cleared lane.

forward accompanied by their regimental antiaircraft troop: open-turreted Crusader tanks mounting twin 20mm Oerlikon guns, ready to support the infantry with direct fire. Advancing along the sunken lane leading through le Vieux Bourg to Sept Vents, five Grenadiers tanks went up in quick succession on mines, two of them blocking the road. Sherman 'Crab' flail tanks of B Squadron, Lothian and Border Yeomanry were called forward towards Sept Vents. The Crabs manoeuvred with difficulty around immobilized Churchills, edging forward at no more than three miles per hour as their drums spun at 180 revolutions per minute. Drivers were blind. The flails beating the ground raised such dense clouds of dust that buttoned-up crews often had only their vacuum-driven gyroscopic direction indicators for guidance, and tank commanders could rarely make out the guiding lights of preceding flailing tanks, much less lines of chalk powder marking the beaten path.[6]

Lieutenant Carter's flails detonated eight mines in less than fifty yards. But as each antitank mine detonated cost another of the flail's forty-three chains, the chances of missing a mine increased. About a dozen mines was the most that could be hoped for, and in this case the ninth mine in the roadside verge blew a track off the tank. Carter called forward the next Crab, Sergeant Rawlinson's, which successfully flailed two mines before being blown up by the simultaneous detonation of a triangle of three mines

35

The approach to Sept Vents village.
Infantry take a break in their advance as tanks roll forward.

set deep in the road. The third tank of the troop abandoned the blocked road and successfully beat a sixteen foot wide lane parallel to the road. (After the action, a roadside machine gun team surrendered from a slit trench positioned to prevent any sappers on foot from clearing the minefield.)

By 08.30 hours, when B Company of the Cameronians reached the

The view north from the German rear over Lutain Wood with the Caumont ridge on the skyline.

village of Sept Vents, only one Churchill tank remained in support, and clearing the village was a slow process until the reserve Churchills of 2 Squadron could be brought forward. Directed by the 2IC (second in command), Lieutenant Colonel Deakin, they overcame the defenders, assisted by the antiaircraft troop which 'had a very good shoot in the village with their Oerlikons'.[7] Finally, by 15.00 hours the Cameronians were able to report Sept Vents clear and ready to receive wheeled transport, C Company and the reserve squadron of tanks forming a protective screen to the south. Cameronians drawing breath amid the ruins were pleased to watch columns of 11th Armoured Division tanks and lorryloads of infantry thundering south west down the Torigni road to cover VIII Corps' open right flank.

On the left, the 2/Gordons advanced through fields and orchards alongside the Cahagnes road towards the wooded valley.[8] Here the leading two companies encountered minefields in front of a network of camouflaged machine gun posts and dug-outs. The Gordons advanced with B Company left and A Company right to establish fire bases on their respective corners of the wood. Each company was supported by two troops of the Grenadiers' 3 Squadron plus an officer in a close-support Churchill tank with its 95mm howitzer. The mines were predominantly antipersonnel, and the Lothians' flails were not needed. But Churchill Crocodile flame-throwing tanks of 141 Regiment RAC ('The Buffs') were on hand and proved their worth as the fight moved into the woods.

With A and B Companies and their accompanying tanks providing

A Churchill Crocodile with its armoured fuel trailer, its crew 'buttoned up' as a precaution against blow-back. The plume of flame from the bow flame projector created a distinctive, black, oily cloud of smoke.

flanking fire, D and then C Companies passed through them into the woods. The supporting Crocodiles of A Squadron, The Buffs advanced to flame the forward German positions. Throughout July, the Buffs' Crocodile tanks had taken steady losses, their surviving crews effectively 'writing the book' of Crocodile tactics as they learned from hard experience. In particular, they had learned the need for supporting fire as they closed to the very short range their flame-throwers required. Nominally this was anything up to a hundred yards, but in reality this was subject to a number of factors, not least wind strength and direction. This morning, as with other tank units in the first wave, there were difficulties caused as much by lack of preparation as by the terrain. Captain Strachan had twice to reorganize his plan as the strength of his two troops fell from six to three tanks, then rose back to four in time for the assault on the Lutain Wood. On arrival, the four Churchill Crocodiles were unable to close in to optimum flaming range due to a high earth bank; nevertheless the flaming had its usual impact on the morale of the defending infantry. The Buffs' War Diary modestly concluded that 'The operation was quite successful'. In fact, their intervention was most effective. It was often impossible for Crocodile crews to distinguish the effects of their own fire from the charred remains of casualties inflicted earlier; and of course the demoralizing effect achieved by flaming the enemy was even harder to measure.

Next, a troop of three Grenadier Guards tanks penetrated the western side of the wood and began firing at the defenders from behind. One of the three Churchills was knocked out, and soon after the troop lieutenant, James Marshall-Cornwall, was killed while directing prisoners towards the advancing

Lieutenant Marshall-Cornwall lies in this quiet corner of Lutain wood. The memorial is found by the side of the D54 road a mile south of Caumont.

The first German prisoners are herded to the rear as a carrier-borne 3-inch mortar platoon hurries forward to secure the ground won.

An infantry officer giving orders by radio from his carrier

Gordons. Unaware of these losses, the troop sergeant's tank remained in the wood. Lance Sergeant Kington's lone tank held its position, firing HE (high explosive) and BESA machine guns into the Germans' rear, at one point liquidating a grenade-throwing German squad at just eight yards range. Opposition slackened.

15th Scottish and 6th Guards Tanks had completed the first phase, and taken prisoner three officers and 148 other ranks of the *752. Infanterie Regiment*. The positions taken were secured, and when the infantry regiments' antitank and mortar platoons were called forward and emplaced on the objectives, the Guards tanks and specialised support armour could be released by the infantry colonels. However the whole operation had fallen far behind timetable. 'X Hour' for phase two of the operation had been set for 09.55 hours, immediately following the heavy bombers' attack. It was now afternoon and phase two had not yet begun. And from 15.55 hours the second and final wave of heavy bombing was due to fall on the day's final objective, still miles away to the south.

THE PUSH SOUTH

The German *326. Division* had received no advance warning of the attack on the morning of Sunday 30th. Of its three component regiments, two were committed to holding a nine mile front. Still believing that they faced resting American units, they were shocked by aerial bombardment, next by the eruption from the Allied lines of fierce Scots infantry and scores of heavy Churchill infantry tanks. Nevertheless, the Germans made the most of their superior tactics and weapons. They resisted fiercely and as their front line positions were being overwhelmed, prepared the local counter attacks called for by German doctrine to recover lost ground before the attacking force could establish on the objective.

Major set-piece British offensives in Normandy frequently underestimated the depth of German defensive positions. Time after time, instead of achieving breakthroughs the British had been slowed by successive defence lines. Stopping to consolidate, British attackers would be thrown back by vigorous local counter attacks. This time, the forward momentum was supposed to be maintained. But the plan was already running late. The Cameronians and Gordons should have cleared the way to the Phase II Start Line, a thousand yards beyond Sept Vents and Lutain Wood, by 09.55 hours. This would be H Hour for the remaining two battalions of 227 Brigade, 10/Highland Light Infantry and 2/Argyll and Sutherland Highlanders, to begin the battle proper.

These two battalions had displaced forward to their Forming Up Places and now waited with impatience. Looking down on the Gordons' fight, the Argylls' commander

> '...began to wonder about 0820 hrs if we should ever get through to cross our S.L. on time.'[9]

So, without waiting for the Lutain Wood struggle to be resolved, the Argylls' two leading companies set off for the Start Line, followed by the 3/Scots Guards' tanks. Similarly, the 10/HLI started down the hill towards Sept Vents supported by 4/Coldstream Guards. To their late start was added the unforeseen difficulty of German defences much deeper than expected. The Argylls' acting commander (Major John Kenneth, in the absence of Colonel J W Tweedie) recorded:

> 'We and the tks started going fwd. Very soon both leading companies reported small arms opposition and it became clear that we were "in the battle" even though our S.L. was still 1500 yards to the SOUTH. The country was close and impassable to carriers and half-tracks, so that difficulty was experienced in keeping touch with higher fmn.'

As usual, the Number 18 infantry wireless sets either were malfunctioning or else their operators were picked off by snipers.

The Argylls finally fought their way to the area of their Start Line around 11.30 hours, but only after encountering considerable resistance. In fact, their Start Line was found to coincide with the enemy's main defended area. Moving up through uncleared ground between Sept Vents and Lutain Wood, losses were taken on minefields and in the confusion companies became separated. The Argylls' Major Kenneth had difficulty

Churchills carrying infantry south of Caumont.

contacting Brigade, and

> '...we found it increasingly difficult for the forward companies of infantry to keep in touch with the tanks, due to the tanks having to jink about and increase speed in order to find crossing places over ditches and hedges. It was not long before we lost sight of the leading squadrons of tanks.'

The major ordered a pause to re-form around Ecorigny, a hamlet in a wooded valley east of Sept Vents:

> 'I considered that by reforming and continuing the advance in good order we would, in the long run, gain time.'

As the battalion reorganised, Kenneth conferred with artillery liaison officers in the hopes of achieving some modification of the artillery concentrations planned for the day (their sequence had been code-named after progressively worse ailments: 'LARYNGITIS', 'MEASLES', 'MUMPS', PLEURISY', 'PNEUMONIA', etc.). Somewhere in the Argylls' right rear the 10/HLI were still struggling forward.

Meanwhile, the two supporting Guards tank battalions (4/Coldstream Guards and 3/Scots Guards) were planning to by-pass the worst obstacles and crash through the German line. This daring move was highly unorthodox and requires some explanation. Churchill tanks were not expected to press on across country without infantry support. Conferring by the fishing tackle shop in Caumont, the infantry's General MacMillan and the tanks' Brigadier Verney discussed next steps. Their assigned role was to cover the right flank of an advancing XXX Corps, but XXX Corps had clearly failed to reach its objectives. The general and the brigadier

Quarry

'Quarry Hill' from the east. The Coldstream Churchills climbed up the sunlit fields. The northern-most German counter attacks were launched from this position.

The quarry today: filled with derelict cars.

The monument commerating the fight for 'Coldstream Hill' beside the busy N175, two miles east of St Martin.

nevertheless determined on a gamble which would if successful keep the VIII Corps plan on track. As Verney later recalled:

'The situation throughout Phase II had been very confused, and my recollections are of many conversations over the air with the two tank battalions, on the rival themes of hurrying on to the objective or staying close to the infantry whose whereabouts were continually uncertain... It was becoming clear that we would never get Phase III off at the rate we were going. It seemed that the only hope was to take a chance and push on alone, and follow up with infantry later as best we could.'[10]

Verney and MacMillan agreed to throw away the book of rules and push the tanks on ahead.

So, reaching the Start Line ahead of the infantry, the Coldstream and the Scots Guards were ordered to press on regardless. Some Glasgow Highlanders arrived just in time to be carried on the backs of Coldstream tanks, but most were left behind so that the tanks might gain some benefit from the pre-planned artillery barrage which was moving on remorselessly a hundred yards every four minutes.

A gamble it certainly was. To the British, it seemed incredible good fortune that the enemy lacked heavy antitank guns. In fact, the overstretched defenders had few of these to deploy, and had decided that the bocage on the Caumont sector was in itself enough to deter vehicles, even fully-tracked tanks. As was so often the case, from the mountains of Tunisia to the forest of the Reichswald, the Churchill tank's extraordinary ability to traverse unfavourable terrain was exploited to the full.[11] So much for the hardware. It is also important to bear in mind the human element. 6th Guards Tank Brigade had trained with 15th Scottish. The tankers had every confidence that 'their' infantry would eventually catch them up, and with this in mind the tanks set off.

TO HILL 309

The right flank story is told first. The Coldstream Churchills rolled straight down the St Martin road. Passing through undefended Hervieux, they could clearly see their objective. Hill 309, 'Quarry Hill', was a dominating peak, midway between the German strongpoint St-Martin-des-Besaces and the towering heights of the Bois du Homme. Already, the hill was being pounded by bombers, its forward slopes erupting in smoke, gouts of earth, and uprooted trees. Near la Morichèse, Major Tollemache's 3 Squadron met a hostile reception in a sunken road:

> *'a real old fashioned home guard ambush – people running about and throwing things amidst the flash of bursting bazooka bombs.'*[12]

His 13 Troop brushed off this ambush but sensing more trouble lurking in the village ahead, he called for smoke to be laid to cover a withdrawal. The troop then moved off-road around the east of the main road, by-passing the village and so avoiding the German 8.8cm gun lying in wait. (This gun was later to account for both the Coldstream's rear-link Churchill and the point tank of the Grenadier Guards' advance, lost along with its burden of Glasgow Highlanders.)

The Coldstream bade their riding Glasgow Highlanders *au revoir*, dropping them off with instructions to 'follow the tank tracks'. The tanks plunged on. The cross country route was not easy, as Major Sir Mark Millbank in command of 2 Squadron recalled:

> *'The high banks, surmounted by scrub, made a cross country ride remarkably uncomfortable! One climbed slowly up the face of a bank, balanced precariously on the top, warned the occupants to hold tight as one launched forth down the other side. In several tanks, men were knocked senseless by the battering.'*

But the Churchills were up to the challenge, as were their drivers, trained in extreme cross country conditions and aware of the often fatal consequences of losing control and turning a Churchill tank over.

Finally, the hill was reached, its lower slopes skirted by a most unwelcome railway cutting. Some tanks shed tracks as they attempted

A 6-pounder antitank gun bringing up the rear to a column of tanks.

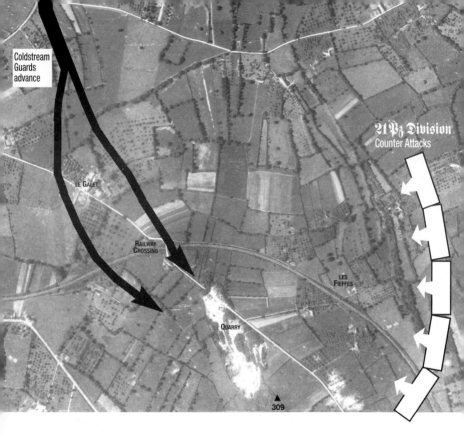

Coldstream
Guards
advance

21 Pz Division
Counter Attacks

LE GALET

RAILWAY
CROSSING

LES
FIEFFES

QUARRY

▲
309

particularly difficult obstacles; others simply found the strain too much for their engines. Lieutenant Cazenove's whole troop became bogged; Sergeant Maughan's tank turned over on its side setting off a grenade inside the turret which severely wounded the three occupants. But the others pressed on upwards. The summit was reached about 16.00 hours. The hill which General Straube had said 'must not be allowed to fall into enemy hands' was abandoned by the Germans. Survivors of the aerial bombardment fled before the totally unlooked-for tanks grinding up the steep slopes.

Though the hold of the Coldstream tanks was tenuous – tanks alone can rarely hold terrain securely – nevertheless the Coldstream remained until the first elements of the 2/Glasgow Highlanders began to arrive from 22.30 hours. By 02.30 hours, the last of the rifle companies was on the hill and the guns of the antitank platoon had been manhandled into place. From the north, the 7/Seaforth of 46 Brigade were on their way to strengthen the position further. Five miles behind the front at the start of the day, Hill 309 was now firmly in British hands. The following morning, Brigadier Verney arrived on the position at 05.00 hours, and triumphantly informed the

46

Coldstream that Hill 309 would henceforth be referred to as 'Coldstream Hill'.

TO HILL 226

Meanwhile to the east, setting off from the vicinity of Lutain Wood, the Scots Guards' Churchills experienced a wild ride: crashing over hedgerows like heavy horses in a steeplechase, spraying whole belts of BESA and putting high explosive rounds into any knots of resistance. The crews were shaken and bruised, commanders struck by low branches and pelted with small, hard cider apples which accumulated on the floors of the tank turrets. Lieutenant Colonel Dunbar records:

> 'We were all black and blue from the jumps we had been over, and quite a number of men, including my signals officer in my tank, had been knocked senseless.'[13]

But the momentum of their daring charge was kept up until they reached their objective of Hill 226 [modern 234]. Behind them, the Argylls were on the move again with a leap-frog advance, alternating fire and movement by companies which carried them rapidly forward in the wake of the tanks. By 15.30 hours, the village of les Loges was secured and B and D companies of 2/A&SH joined their armoured friends on the slopes of Hill 226. The infantry dug in on the northern reverse slope while the tanks adopted hull-down positions on the crestline.

At 16.00 hours, the Argylls' commander judged that his battalion was established on the objective. Normally this would have been the time to release the supporting tanks. However, the Argylls' organic antitank support, a platoon of six 6-pounder guns, was still struggling forward through les Loges. The position was extremely exposed. Although Hill 309

Churchills moving up to rendezvous with infantry during the offensive.

to the south west was now occupied by tanks, that flank was by no means secure. And to the east, where XXX Corps' 43rd Division should by this time have been established on the Bois du Homme massif, very little progress had been made since morning. The left flank of the breakthrough remained wide open. So, it was agreed between the Argylls' Major Kenneth and the Guards' Lieutenant Colonel Dunbar that the tanks would stay on with the infantry. This was reinforced by orders from 6th Tank Brigade to hold the hill and les Loges 'at all costs'. As the Jocks deepened their slit trenches, repaired radios were tuned to the BBC 6 o'clock news, whose main story was their own big attack and the capture of Sept Vents.

JAGDPANTHERS ON HILL 226

Around 18.30 hours, the peace was shattered by a heavy artillery 'stonk', catching Guardsmen out of their tanks while their officers gathered for an 'O Group' briefing. One tank was hit twice in succession, its commander Captain Beeson dying as he tried to aid his wounded co-driver. In their slit trenches and from their Churchill tanks, the defenders of Hill 226 faced south towards the dominating wooded ridge of the Bois du Homme, preparing to receive a counter attack.

Both the form and the direction of the attack were unexpected. Within moments, all three Churchill tanks of Lieutenant Cunningham's troop, the easternmost on the hill, were destroyed, the lieutenant being severely wounded. From the north east of the hill, there emerged two massive German self-propelled antitank guns. These were *Jagdpanther* of *3. Kompanie, schwere Panzerjäger Abteilung 654*, hastily called forward to support the crumbling *326 Infanterie Division*. As the two advanced, a third in an overwatch position gave covering fire.

Each of these monsters mounted a long 8.8cm PaK43/3, a gun easily capable of destroying any tank in the Allied arsenal, with precision optics that frequently achieved a kill with the first shot fired. This forty-five ton

A third *Jagdpanther* in overwatch gave covering fire.

Panels of appliqué armour have been welded to these Sherman IIs (M4A1) (23/Hussars) as added protection from the dreaded 88s.

vehicle was propelled by a 23 litre Maybach engine delivering 700 brake horsepower. The Churchills were a similar weight but by contrast had a Bedford lorry's engine developing 350 horsepower. Unsurprisingly, the *Jagdpanther's* maximum speed of twenty-eight miles per hour was twice the Churchill's.

A skilled *Panzerjäger* commander chose his positions and sited his guns before combat. *Leutnant* Scheiber had been ordered to take his platoon (1. *Zug* of 3. *Kompanie*) of three *Jagdpanther* forward to support the hard-pressed infantry. (Some British observers reported only two attackers; German records confirm that Scheiber commanded three *Jagdpanther* in this action.)[14] Stopping in a sunken road, Scheiber had dismounted to reconnoitre ahead with one of his commanders. *Unteroffizier* Richarz recalls:

>*'Twenty minutes passed, then he returned, smiling. They had counted eight enemy tanks. The engines roared and our tank destroyers rumbled forward through shell craters and hedges... The Tommies sat on and beside the tanks, smoking, as if they were at a training area.'*[15]

Keeping their thick frontal armour faced towards the enemy, all three *Jagdpanther* came at the British, alternately moving and firing, destroying a Scots Guards' Churchill with almost every round fired:

>*'We were jubilant; we had knocked out the first enemy tank in the company. Round after round left the barrel. One after another they went up in flames. By this time the Tommies in one tank were in a panic. They abandoned their vehicle and ran into some vegetation. We fired at them with high-explosive rounds and machine guns. Hunting fever had gripped all of us.'*[16]

The Scots Guards position on Hill 226.

The Scots Guards arrived in France confident in the thick armour of their heavy infantry tanks, but confidence soon evaporated as they visited a 'tank graveyard' and witnessed the damage a German 7.5cm antitank gun could inflict, even on a Churchill. And the impact of a round from an 8.8cm gun was even more catastrophic. No less daunting was the realisation of what happened inside a Churchill when it was hit and burned. Feverish attempts were made to weld spare track links onto turrets and hulls. Official reports dismissed this as futile or worse, leading only to the further overloading of the heavy Churchill tanks. In the case of the lighter Sherman tanks, there is some evidence that the extra panels of 'appliqué armour' hastily welded to the sides covering the ammunition racks, were actually used as aiming points by German gunners. But the practice was

allowed to continue as it might give the confidence of the British tank crews some small boost. This was sorely needed. Tank crews lived in fear of German '88s'. Of the Normandy campaign, the 6th Guards Tank Brigade history records:

> 'Every member of the Brigade knew that his passport to heaven was engraved with a large 88.'[17]

A Churchill had no realistic chance of defeating a *Jagdpanther's* frontal armour. The Scots Guards had already converted most (possibly all) of their 6-pounder-armed Mark IV Churchills to 75mm guns, which had somewhat reduced armour penetrating capability and would do scant damage to the front of a *Jagdpanther*. More experienced units in Normandy had already seen the need to set aside the conversion kits and to use the remaining 6-pounder-armed Churchills to lead the way in action, ideally with one of the new APDS (armour-piercing, discarding-sabot) rounds 'up the spout'. But such precautions were irrelevant where the frontal armour of a *Jagdpanther* was concerned. As other Churchill units were to discover in the days to come, even 6-pounder 'sabot' rounds bounced off a *Jagdpanther's* glacis plate 'like ping-pong balls'.[18] As the campaign in north west Europe progressed, some British tank units came to prefer to use high explosive rounds (HE) against large German tanks: while there was little chance of penetration, HE rounds might be mistaken for artillery fire which, with luck, could cause Panther or Tiger tanks to pull back.

The Germans rolled through the Scots Guards, leaving a trail of wrecked Churchill tanks. Captain William Whitelaw, commanding S Squadron, was in his scout car back with his reserve troop when

> *'...the mortaring and shelling on the hill suddenly intensified. Then I saw the left hand tank of my left forward troop go up in flames closely followed by the other two. Immediately I started to return to the hill. As I was driving up the field I saw all three tanks of my left flank troop go up in flames, and as I approached the top of the hill, I saw a tank moving from right to left in front of me. Suddenly it appeared to me (wearing a headset) as if the turret of this tank had been quietly lifted off and put down on the ground some yards away.'*[19]

One German commander was observed standing in his hatch, laughing at the scene and giving a mock salute as the three monsters roared off the hill.

One observer was critical of the German tactics. Charles Farrell, 2IC of Left Flank Squadron in his close-support Churchill, remains convinced that the German commander:

> *'...threw away a dominating fire position by his ill-advised charge'.*

He maintained that:

> *'Had they been better trained and better commanded they would have held their position at the edge of the wood and engaged Right Flank Squadron with what might well have been similar devastating results.'*[20]

It is true that, for all its awesome strength, the *Jagdpanther* was not an assault gun. Its role was defensive, as a tank destroyer, ideally firing from cover and out of range of the tanks it destroyed. Still, from the German perspective, *Leutnant* Scheiber was held up as an example of decisive leadership, praised for such unorthodox practices as leading his guns into action on a motorcycle, and even at times taking over the gunner's position within his own vehicle. The German army had different views about inspirational leadership. It should be noted that on the Russian front, equipped with the Ferdinand self-propelled antitank gun which lacked any defensive machine gun, elements of 654. *Abteilung* had occasionally plunged into Russian positions relying on shock and noise alone to frighten off enemy infantry.

With the Argylls' own 6-pounder antitank guns and attached Royal

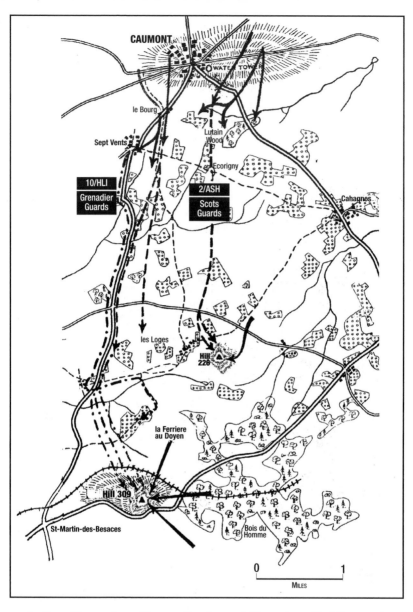

Artillery 17-pounders still struggling forward, Kenneth recalled 'It proved to be an armour show and there was little that the infantry could do about it'. Ron Lomas' 6-pounder gun arrived on the scene about 19.00 hours and was waiting for orders at the corner of a field, with a clear view of the hillside dotted with wrecked Churchill tanks. Along the hedgerow approached a Guardsman, bareheaded and shocked:

> 'He was on his hands and knees; he wouldn't get up for anything. He

53

shouted to us, "Don't go up there, it's murder!" '

Before the scene was obscured by a British smoke barrage, whose shells fell perilously close to the antitank guns' ammunition carriers, some of the men spotted German vehicles withdrawing.

After dark, the tanks fell back from the hill to a 'Forward Rally' on the eastern edge of les Loges. A hot meal was prepared but most men were too tired to eat. The Padre's party did the rounds of the wrecked tanks. Twelve S Squadron Churchills had been knocked out, in addition to the tank of the regimental 2IC, Major Cuthbert, whose destruction Captain Whitelaw had witnessed. Its thickest frontal armour had been cleanly penetrated and its turret torn off in the resulting explosion. So violent was the conflagration that the men's identity discs were never found so the crew had to be reported 'missing'.

Some days later, two of the three *Jagdpanther* were found abandoned, including Scheiber's own vehicle '311', blown up by its crew after suffering transmission breakdown, possibly caused by 75mm HE hits to the suspension from the tank of Right Flank Squadron's Liaison Captain. But that night on Hill 226, even this small consolation was lacking. The Right Flank 2IC, Captain Charles Farrell went forward with his co-driver to seek the *Jagdpanther*. They walked forward half a mile but, 'finding nothing – not even tank tracks – returned to the Squadron'.[21]

References

1 *Sherwood Rangers*, T M Lindsay, 1952, ISBN 0-947828-20-6, p 108.

2 *Reflections 1939-1945 A Scots Guards Officer in Training and War*, Charles Farrell, 2000, ISBN 1-85821-761-X, p 54-58.

3 Martin, p 81.

4 *Infantry Colonel*, Brigadier George Taylor, 1990, ISBN 1-854421-085-8, p 54-55.

5 *The History of the Cameronians (Scottish Rifles) Volume III 1933-1946*, Brigadier C N Barclay, 1947.

6 *Achtung! Minen!: The Making of a Flail Tank Commander*, Ian C Hammerton, 1991, ISBN 0-86332-533-5, p 51-59; *Sherman: A History of the American Medium Tank*, R P Hunnicutt, 1978, p 444.

7 British Army of the Rhine BLUECOAT Battlefield Tour, 1947, Lieutenant Colonel C M F Deakin, 2IC 4 Tk Gren Gds.

8 *The Life of a Regiment Volume IV 1919-1945 The History of the Gordon Highlanders*, Wilfrid Miles, 1961, ISBN 0-7232-2785-3

9 BAOR Battlefild Tour, Major John Kenneth, 2A&SH

10 BAOR Battlefield Tour, Major General G L Verney, 6 GDS TK BDE

11 Mr. Churchill's Tank: *The British Infantry Tank Mark IV*, David Fletcher, 1999, ISBN 0-7643-0679-0, p 109 & 150-151

12 BAOR Battlefield Tour, Major J E Tollemache, 3 Sqn 4 Tk COLDM GDS

13 BAOR Battlefield Tour, Lieutenant Colonel C I H Dunbar, 3 TK SG

14 *The Combat History of Schwere Panzerjäger Abteilung 654*, Karlheinz Münch, 2002, ISBN 0-921991-60-6, p 372.

15 Münch, p 337.

16 Münch, p 337.

17 6th Guards Tank Brigade: The Story of Guardsmen in Churchill Tanks, Patrick Forbes, 1946, p6

18 Forbes, p 24

19 BAOR Battlefield Tour, Captain W S I Whitelaw, S SQN 3 TK SG

20 Farrell, p 83

21 Farrell, 83-84

CHAPTER FOUR

Monday 31 July –
DICKIE'S BRIDGE

PROBING FOR GAPS

The Normandy road network made few concessions to the needs of a
modern army, and traffic jams were an inescapable part of every British
offensive there. Their mobility hindered, 11th Armoured Division's tank-
infantry battle groups had been frustrated in their objectives. By nightfall
on 30 July, the 3/RTR and 8/Rifle Brigade group had stopped short of their
intended St-Martin-des-Besaces, around the abandoned village of la
Morichèse. The 2/Fife and Forfar Yeomanry and 4/Kings Shropshire Light
Infantry had stopped around Dampierre. And between these two flanks,

**The Normandy road network made few concessions to the needs
of a modern army.**

the 23/Hussars and 3/Monmouths group had actually been counter attacked by a German regiment with some assault gun support at St-Jean-des-Essartiers.

Behind the lines waited the divisional armoured car regiment: 2/Household Cavalry, the Royal Horse Guards. Only after midnight were their reconnaissance squadrons ordered forward, joining the queues of vehicles negotiating the white taped lanes through the minefields and the ruins of Caumont. From dawn, they began their specialist job, probing for weak spots in the enemy lines east and west of the German stronghold of St Martin.

Put simply, the job of a reconnaissance unit was to drive beyond the front lines to locate the enemy. In Normandy this usually meant driving until fired upon. A former armoured car officer (of 11/Hussars) recalled that the role of the leading car of the troop was:

'...to drive straight on until some German gunner took a shot. On every one of these mornings, in the chill and damp of a half-darkness which heralded a nineteen-hour day, the driver of each car would lower himself into his seat and the crew would pile in afterwards, all knowing that their chances of survival rested on the aim of the first German gun or tank they might encounter.'[1]

Car commanders travelled with eyes peeled for signs of trouble, ready to trigger the smoke dispensers at a moment's notice, and most often keeping a grenade within easy reach.

THE HOUSEHOLD CAVALRY

One troop of Household Cavalry had already ventured into St Martin from the north, and lost its two leading cars. Another car taking a wrong turning and entering the town from the east was shot to pieces. From then on, St Martin was subjected to a concentric attack by 11th Armoured's tank and infantry regiments, while the cavalry looked elsewhere for alternative routes south. Time after time, a car rounding a bend would run into enemy infantry, or assault guns of the newly arriving 21 Panzerdivision. The drill was well rehearsed: all cars would fire their smoke dischargers and reverse at top speed, the lead car always hoping that those behind would react quickly enough to get out of the way.

Approaching Cauville, a hamlet on the main road leading west out of St Martin, 1 Troop of C Squadron lost two of its four cars, immobilised in a narrow lane. This left a Daimler Dingo scout car and the troop commander Lieutenant Derek ('Dickie') Powle in a heavy Staghound armoured car. These two cars dashed across the main St Martin to Villedieu road, only to find themselves in the midst of a German antiaircraft battery. Before the guns could respond, the cars used surprise and speed to pass straight though the position. Now Powle judged it safer to press on forwards than

The American built M6 (Chevrolet) Staghound with a 37mm gun.

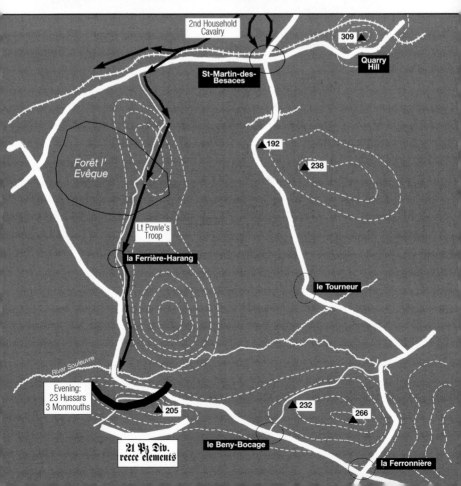

2nd Household Cavalry

309

Quarry Hill

St-Martin-des-Besaces

Forêt l' Evêque

192

238

Lt Powle's Troop

la Ferrière-Harang

le Tourneur

River Souleuvre

Evening: 23 Hussars 3 Monmouths

205

232

266

21 Pz Div. recce elements

le Beny-Bocage

la Ferronnière

The two cars motored on into the dark woods.

to retrace their way through an alerted enemy, shouting ahead to Corporal Bland in the Dingo:

'We may as well try what's in front; it can't be worse than trying to neck it back through that lot!'

So the two cars motored on, down a minor road leading into an area of heavily wooded hills, the Forêt l'Evêque. The road twisted and turned through the dark, eerily-silent forest. Eventually the cars emerged into the open, passed through the small town of la Ferrière-Harang, and carried on southwards, still without encountering any substantial opposition. At one point, a German four-wheeled armoured car appeared ahead, and Powle's two cars followed for some distance – close behind but partially hidden by its dust. They did not cause the German car any apparent alarm, and enemy observers would have assumed that the three vehicles were a single German column, British vehicles in German use being a common sight.

DICKIE'S BRIDGE

Shortly after the German four-wheeler turned off the road, a bridge appeared ahead of the British cars. The steep sided valley of the River Souleuvre was a major obstacle, and the bridge an unexpected prize. Corporal Bland recalls,

'It was decided that I should have a crack at crossing it, covered by the armoured car. It worked, and after quickly dismounting we (myself and Trooper Read) slipped up behind a German sentry and quietly finished him off. We had to dispose of any such visitors, otherwise we were sunk as there was no hope of holding off any numbers with only two cars.'

The Staghound crossed in its turn and both vehicles went into cover in the trees within sight of the bridge. As the crews set about camouflaging the vehicles, Corporal Staples, the Staghound gunner/operator worked the radio.

The principal weapon of Dickie Powle's troop was its radio. Information from behind enemy lines could potentially wreak far more havoc than the Staghound's small 37mm cannon. But as with any weapon, range was a factor, and the

Dickie Powle's first view of the Souleuvre crossing.

combination of distance and rolling wooded terrain made contact very difficult. Six miles away, 2/Household Cavalry headquarters was struggling to make contact with cars much closer than Powle's. The mush of carrier waves was interrupted by lengthy ramblings from VIII Corps HQ, and periodically drowned by a high-powered American transmitter over which an operator calling himself 'Blackboid' would intone, 'I can

The bridge with modern solar panel for illumination.

hear you now, fine and dandy'.[2]

Staples had to transmit over and over again before he made contact. Finally, he got off the vital message:

'At 10.30 hours the bridge at 637436 is clear of enemy and still intact. I say again, at 10.30 hours the bridge at 637436 is clear of enemy and still intact.'

When the reference was found to be so far beyond any known penetration of enemy lines, Colonel Abel Smith was incredulous and demanded an instant repeat. Back came the confirmation. 11th Armoured had won a bridge over the Souleuvre.

Different accounts of Corporal Staples' radio transmission give varying co-ordinates: 637436 was the true position of the bridge. The actual location of this bridge is known as 'les Vaux de Souleuvre', near a farm itself called 'Souleuvre'. The modern plaque on the bridge calls it 'le Pont du Taureau' after the 11th Armoured Division's 'Black Bull' insignia; 'Pip' Roberts on more than one occasion refers to it as simply 'the bridge'! To avoid confusion with other Souleuvre crossings, this bridge will hereafter be referred to as it became known at the time: 'Dickie's Bridge'.

The story goes that a staff officer congratulated 'Pip' Roberts on securing the bridge with the words, 'Why, sir, two men and a boy could have held you up there'. To which Roberts is supposed to have replied, 'Yes, Joe, but they didn't have the boy'. Why such a strategic bridge was so lightly guarded was a mystery soon resolved. Dickie Powle's tiny force had

They sprayed the place with BESA.

run directly along a boundary between two German corps, only established during the preceding night. The boundaries between units are typically points of weakness. Both Meindl's *II Fallschirmjäger Korps* to the west and Straube's *LXXIV Armee Korps* to the east were stretched thin. Neither had seen fit to allocate precious resources to the defence of the densely wooded Forêt l'Evêque. Each formation chose to assume that the other bore responsibility for this strip of land, and neither sent troops in. Later in the day, a *21 Panzerdivision* despatch rider was ambushed at the bridge, and using codes found on him, British Second Army deciphered radio exchanges between the commanders of the adjacent German 3 *Fallschirmjâger Division* and 326 *Infanterie Division*. Each accused the other of neglecting the boundary. But it was too late for recriminations; the damage was done.

The news of the bridge was rushed to Division HQ, and new plans were prepared to exploit the unforeseen opportunity. The first priority was to reinforce the five men at the Souleuvre crossing. Soon on the way was a group from the 2/Northants Yeomanry, the Cromwell tank regiment of 11th Armoured. The Yeomanry had had a quiet start to BLUECOAT, posted on the far right flank as a link with the American 5th Division. Now engaged, and taking losses, to the west of St Martin, the Yeomanry despatched two troops – six Cromwell tanks – to the bridge. These tanks encountered opposition as they passed through la Ferrière-Harang and were briefly held up. Being less shy than the armoured cars, they sprayed the place with BESA. As they fought, they were joined by the four cars of the Household Cavalry's 5 Troop, D Squadron under Lieutenant Bethell. Seeing the hold-up, the Household Cavalry troop tried another forest road, leading west. Shortly after, they went off the air and were not heard from again. Their four burnt out cars were found the following day. The Cromwells pressed on to the bridge, where they arrived, to everyone's great relief, about 14.00 hours.

More substantial forces followed, in the shape of 23/Hussars and 3/Monmouths. These disengaged with some difficulty from the fight around St Martin and by mid afternoon were on their way. Rather than attempt the narrow track through the Forêt l'Evêque, they took a longer route on wider roads. This, as 'Pip' Roberts admitted, 'was not a big success'. The column passed around the north of the forest, intending to make a left turn onto the road from Torigni-sur-Vire. Unfortunately, they found the road was already in use.

THE DISPUTED BOUNDARY

In the American sector, General Leonard Gerow's V Corps risked being left behind, 'squeezed out' between the American

General Gerow

British infantry march past Americans as a despatch rider debates who has the right of way.

XIX Corps on their right approaching Vire from the west and the British VIII Corps on their left coming down from the north. On 28 July the Germans in front of Gerow – *General der Fallschirmjäger* Eugen Meindl's *II Fallschirmjäger Korps* – were given permission to fall back, and the following day Gerow directed his three division commanders to follow. Gerow's *2 Division* received his orders:

'By-pass everything. Never mind these little pockets of resistance. Let's get down and take a bath in the Vire!'

By 31 July, the most promising advances were being made by Gerow's left flank 5 Division, closest to the British. Unable to find the division's general, Gerow personally telephoned a regimental commander to tell him to mount his infantry on tanks and move fast. 'In short, hurry!'[3]

As Gerow spoke, 23/Hussars were disputing with elements of the US 5th Division the use of the road south of Torigni. Less than an hour after his telephone call, Gerow was informed, and he reacted angrily:

'Well now, I don't like British walking across our front taking [our] objectives.'

In fact, permission had been asked and granted for the British advance, but Gerow was unaware. 'Pip' Roberts was brought into the dispute and recorded:

'Every possible channel was used to defuse the situation and finally someone on the ground was able to point out that "their" bridge was a couple of miles over on the right and then all was peace between us.'

Nevertheless, confusion had been caused; the advance of both Americans and British was disrupted.

The Hussars were redirected back through the forest where to their great surprise:

> '...the Forêt l'Evêque, a perfect defensive position, was completely clear of Germans, and this lent strength to our growing conviction that we were now through the main defensive line. We determined to move on at all speed... It was a tonic to everyone to be able to push forward into France

The first experience of liberation.

The wood-lined road climbed up from the bridge.

without fighting every mile of the way, as we had grown used to doing.'[4]
A further tonic awaited. Emerging from the Forêt l'Evêque, 23/Hussars
had their first experience of celebrating the liberation of a French village as
they passed through the excited folk of la Ferrière-Harang. Hitherto, the
Hussars like many British units had been somewhat disappointed by the
reception given them by Norman countryfolk. For many of these, the cost
of 'liberation' had been lost homes and livelihoods. Now, the 23/Hussars'
historian recalls:

> *'We received the long-awaited flowers and cups of cider, handed to us
> by delighted French girls, and we had our first taste of the cheering and
> jubilation which was to be our normal lot during our advance that
> autumn.'*

Just as things threatened to get out of hand, a sudden explosion sent the
townsfolk running back to their homes. The noise was caused by B
Squadron engaging some Germans on the road out of the town; seeing a
German artillery piece, Major Wigan had swung his turret so quickly that
his accompanying Monmouths company commander was flung into a
ditch. The Hussars tanks, loaded with Monmouths infantry, resumed the
journey to the bridge.

HUSSARS AND MONMOUTHS

The Hussars and Monmouths began to arrive at the Souleuvre Bridge about 21.00 hours. The armoured car and Cromwell crews declared the road ahead up the wooded valley to be clear and the Hussars' B Squadron began to cross. The crossing was briefly halted by an explosion that wounded two Monmouths riding on the back of a Sherman tank. The rest of B Squadron laid smoke, then followed by the infantry plunged into the wooded hills south of the bridge, intent on locating the enemy. In fact, the explosion on the bridge was later discovered to have been caused by a PIAT round 'cooking off' on a hot engine cover. (PIAT rounds were notoriously unstable – not for nothing did the British Army prohibit unathorized firing of the weapon immediately the war was over!) B Squadron soon found real enemies in the form of a German vehicle (reportedly a self-propelled gun towing a trailer, possibly a half-track belonging to the reconnaissance regiment of *21. Panzerdivision*) which was fired upon and withdrew with its trailer burning.

Meanwhile, C Squadron had continued up the narrow road in the hope of pushing on through the night towards le Bény-Bocage. Lieutenant Bishop of the leading troop recalls:

> 'On this occasion the entire Second Army advance is being led by these two Squadrons... This is a most nerve-wracking operation, as the road twists and turns, and one never knows from one moment to the next whether something is going to open up at point blank range, without any warning.'

Some way above the bridge, the road emerged from the woods allowing a commanding view north over the valley, though the wooded ridge still loomed to the right. From this point, Bishop's lead tank, commanded by Sergeant Dixon:

> '...is moving cautiously forward and I have halted on the bend just behind, with guns loaded, and everything ready for action. Suddenly, without any warning, there is a flash and a cloud of black smoke envelopes Dixon's tank.'[5]

Three mines had detonated together, destroying the tank and slewing it broadside-on to block the narrow road. Bishop's tank covered the surviving crew as they assisted the limping Sergeant Dixon back down the road.

By the time a pioneer section arrived to inspect the mines, it was getting dark. Bishop and the officer of engineers walked forward to the wreck, still burning though its radio continued to hum and its pilot light illuminated the blackened turret. All exits from the narrow track were found festooned with mines and the work of clearance began. At length, Bishop was able to advance his own tank past the wreck, wearing an old German infantry helmet and squinting over the turret into the darkness as German machine gun fire sent the pioneers back into the woods. Finally, and to his undisguised relief, the advance to le Bény-Bocage was called off and Bishop rejoined the rest of C Squadron about midnight. B Squadron likewise threaded their way back through the woods to spend the night in the tight regimental leaguer around the bridgehead. Higher up, the British infantry dug in on the wooded slopes.

The day had seen confusion on both sides. For Allies as well as Germans, misunderstandings over unit boundaries were to be a major factor in the development of the campaign. For the Germans, the damage was done and the loss of the Souleuvre bridge was going to unravel the defence plan for the entire Saint Martin – Bois du Homme sector. On balance, the Allies had so far profited from confusion, but the question of the Allied inter-Army boundary was to come up again, and was to limit the ultimate success of Operation BLUECOAT.

Reference

1 *Berlin or Bust: Wartime Life with the 11th Hussars,* Keith Osborne, 2000, p 71.

2 *Caen: Anvil of Victory,* Alexander McKee, 1964, p 334.

3 Blumenson, p 291-294

4 *The Story of the Twenty-Third Hussars, 1940-1946,* 1946, p 87.

5 *The Battle: a Tank Officer Remembers,* Geoffrey S C Bishop, p 67 (note: some dates given in this work need to be treated with caution.)

CHAPTER FIVE

Tuesday 1 August –
DAY OF BREAKTHROUGH

HIGH COMMAND

Day three of BLUECOAT was to prove decisive for both high commands. Dempsey and Montgomery could see that the lead XXX Corps was making little progress, while VIII Corps had achieved its objectives and then erupted into the German rear areas. The whole emphasis of the operation was switched; from this point on, BLUECOAT was an VIII Corps show.

Meanwhile von Kluge's nightmare continued. Rational analysis indicated that the American breakthrough was unlikely to be contained, but contrary to all military logic, the *Führer* insisted on holding the line.

General of the *Waffen* SS Paul Hausser, the first SS general ever to command a whole army, was sticking to the party line and playing down the strategic significance of developments on his Seventh Army front:

> *'Only armoured elements have broken through – so far there has been no exploitation of the breakthrough with massed forces.'*

This effectively echoed the blind faith and impossible fantasies emanating from the *Führerhauptquartier*. Hitler thundered:

> *'We must not get bogged down with mopping up the Americans who have broken through,'*

Nevertheless, Hausser was still screaming to Kluge for reinforcements. Kluge certainly did recognize the gravity of the situation. The American breakthrough threatened the whole Normandy front. Kluge saw that *Panzer Group West* held the 'hinge' of the Normandy defence; if there were to be a strategic withdrawal, the German Army Group B would pivot around Vire, using the crucial roads eastward from that town. And this was the very sector where, directly in front of the British VIII Corps, Straube's *LXXIV Korps* was crumbling.

SS-*Oberstgruppenführer* Paul Hausser

BRITISH TANK-INFANTRY TACTICS

Although achieved by tanks and footsoldiers briefly separated, the breakthrough south of Caumont was nevertheless an illustration of infantry and 'infantry tanks' working together in harmony. The history of the 15th Scottish records that their success on the first day of BLUECOAT was largely due to the 'previous and intimate co-operation' of 6th Guards Tanks, 'old friends' of the division. The history of the 6th goes further, acknowledging:

'It was an act of providence which ordained that the 6th Guards Tank Brigade should go into their own first battle with their old friends... Had the infantry been strangers, the tanks would not have advanced alone so far.'

The close terrain of Normandy made tanks and infantry mutually dependent. The Germans had developed suppressive machine gun fire and sniping to a fine art; tank support could make all the difference. But a new generation of German hand-held antitank weapons made unaccompanied tanks terribly vulnerable. Tanks in close country were deaf

Generalfeldmarschall Günter von Kluge recognised the seriousness of the penetration by the Americans.

A new generation of infantry antitank weapons. One soldier has a *Panzerschreck* rocket launcher over his left shoulder, another has a *Panzerfaust* over his right and two *Panzerschreck* rockets hanging from his belt.

Infantry company and tank squadron commanders confer.

to all but radio messages and virtually blind as well.[1] The tank commander had only a narrow field of vision through his periscopes, unless he risked exposing the top of his head for a better view (most did just that and many paid the ultimate price). Without previously agreed plans and signals, it is very hard for a man on foot to communicate with a tank. One infantry officer desperate for tank support recalled being ignored by a sergeant commanding a Churchill tank:

> 'I felt really wild, but there was nothing I could do to stop him as he went out of earshot, short of firing a round past his ear with my rifle which would probably have only made him close the hatch.'[2]

In 11th Armoured's first action, Scots infantrymen had complained bitterly that the tanks whose support they craved remained 'closed down and deaf to all our appeals'. Even later when telephones were mounted on the outside of the tanks, these were not linked to the vehicle crew's intercom, and the chances of a tank crew 'answering the telephone' in the heat of battle were slim.

As previously noted, by late July 'Pip' Roberts' 11th Armoured had absorbed the lesson that infantry and tanks needed to work together. Their success in BLUECOAT and after was in part the consequence of the flexible organization Roberts introduced. In place of a division composed of a brigade of tanks and one of infantry:

> *'It was my intention to have two brigades each containing two armoured regiments and two infantry battalions... it must be entirely flexible... and the brigadiers themselves must be prepared to operate as armoured brigadiers or infantry brigadiers.'*[3]

Roberts had encouraged the sharing of lessons learned from earlier actions. In answer to problems encountered in Normandy, specific co-operation procedures were agreed. For example, when faced with an enemy-held Norman village, 11th Armoured Division decreed:

> *'It will be normal for a Motor Coy to be under comd of the Armd Regt concerned. This Motor Company will be netted on the Regt Comd Net. Its carriers should move as close behind the tks as possible and in any event not more than 500 yds. The motor pls should move 500 yds behind the carriers. Tks will penetrate the outskirts of the village probably before arrival of inf in order to protect themselves from AP fire from the flanks and one or two tps will be prepared to penetrate the village with inf. Close liaison between tp and pl comds will be essential. Only very limited objectives in the village will be taken on. The remainder of the regt will take up suitable posns in the outskirts of the village and will be relieved as soon as possible by a troop of SP A.Tk guns, placed under comd and netted to the motor company.'*

This was not the way 11th Armoured had fought battles like EPSOM, where Roberts had ruefully observed, the infantry and the armour 'rather went their separate ways'.

One practical – and important! – detail was: given leaders of equal rank, who commanded a mixed force, the infantry or the armour officer present? This is where training and familiarity were invaluable. Major 'Ned' Thornburn (of 4/KSLI) recorded 11th Armoured Division's solution:

> *'This organization was to be entirely flexible and any armoured regiment had to be prepared to work with any infantry battalion. Similarly the two Brigadiers... had to be prepared to command armour and infantry together. Which CO was in overall command of an infantry/armoured group would depend on the situation – in practice this never seemed to present any problem to us since everyone just got on with his job of working with his opposite number.'*[4]

This was easier said than done. But by the end of July, the intention was being put into practice.

The 23/Hussars' historian records:

> *'The Third Monmouths were to be our colleagues and our time together was a very successful one... There is no doubt that in that bocage country the infantryman had to do the lion's share of the work, and right well they did it.'*[5]

In such close country it was difficult enough for a troop leader to keep track of the whereabouts of the three tanks accompanying his own, to say

'We assume quite a different appearance with these men clinging to our vehicles.'

nothing of spotting a lone, *Panzerfaust*-toting enemy infantryman. Another 23/Hussars history records how the Hussars-Monmouths group worked during BLUECOAT:

> *'The infantry are waiting for us. They are all dressed in light marching order, with camouflage over their tin helmets, and carrying rifles, sten guns, Brens, and all the usual impedimenta of the infantry soldier... The various platoons sort themselves out, climbing on the back of our tanks. There is a rough-and-ready all-round defence arrangement with the men on the outside of the vehicle, suitably armed ready to deal with immediate trouble and ready to dismount at a moment's notice. In each case, an Infantry Officer goes on the Troop Leader's tank. We assume quite a different appearance with these men clinging to our vehicles, but somehow we take heart from each other.'*[6]

Although in time to become standard procedure, in the British Army of July 1944 such co-operation was exceptional. Historically, the British Army emphasis on regimental tradition fostered an independence which ran contrary to co-operation, especially co-operation between the different arms of infantry and cavalry. For the Guards, with particularly exclusive regimental traditions, the idea was revolutionary. An infantryman with Guards Armoured Division, Major Wilson joined 3/Irish Guards on 3 August. Yet only a month later, in Belgium, did his platoon get 'our first close-up view of a tank'. He reflected later,

> *'It seems surprising that, for infantry in an armoured division, training in Britain did not include any exercises in company with tanks.'*

And throughout the Normandy campaign 'we operated separately as

71

armour and infantry'. As late as September he was reflecting:

> 'My otherwise excellent infantry training had not prepared me what to expect in close company with armour.'[7]

Guards Armoured Division's own history states:

> 'It should be recalled that the close and constant working together of armoured and infantry units and sub-units had only developed as a result of experience during the campaign. It had only been practised in England at all during the last few weeks of training on the Wolds and even then it had not been anticipated that the relationship would be nearly so intimate as in fact it became.'[8]

Dominick Graham commanded a battery of the West Somerset Yeomanry, the towed 25-pounder field regiment of Guards Armoured Division. He observed about his division:

> 'I never saw infantry and armour working together in England. The infantry brigade and the armoured brigade were expected to work separately. The general idea was that the infantry made the gap and then the armour flooded through it like the cavalry of old.'[9]

This was not the way to succeed in the close terrain south of Caumont.

ENTER THE GUARDS

On 31 July, with the fall of St-Martin-des-Besaces to 11th Armoured imminent, General O'Connor called forward Guards Armoured from their reserve position north of Caumont:

> 'The Guards Armoured Division will move forward immediately through Caumont to St-Martin-des-Besaces and drive south to seize the le Tourneur bridge over the Souleuvre by nightfall.'

With 11th Armoured increasingly committed to a wide right-hook manoeuvre across Dickie's Bridge, the Guards would take responsibility for punching a vital second bridgehead for VIII Corps' advance south. The divisional task was to move through St Martin and advance to le Tourneur, then on across the Souleuvre River to the Bény-Bocage ridge. Thereafter, the division would go on to move in parallel with 11th Armoured on its right, on the axis St-Charles-de-Percy, Montchamp, Estry. In turn, 15th Scottish would cover the Guards' left.

There was a rider to the Guards' orders. General O'Connor was aware of – and impressed by – Pip Roberts' reorganization of 11th Armoured. Indeed, so impressed was he that he took the idea for his own. When O'Connor directed Roberts that 'You must be prepared for the very closest of tank/infantry co-operation on a troop/platoon basis,' Roberts recognised the order as a seal of approval on the organisation he had already set in place. O'Connor then assumed that Guards Armoured would be able to emulate their sister division's flexibility. Newly arrived in the Caumont area on 31 July, Guards Armoured was just beginning to

Guardsmen south of Caumont taking cover.

enjoy the local scenery, largely untouched by the ravages of war, when O'Connor dropped his bombshell. Over luncheon on 31 July, General O'Connor held a conference at which he informed the division of a new regrouping of its battalions, to take place immediately. The three armoured battalions of 5th Guards Armoured Brigade were to 'pair off' with the three infantry battalions of 32nd Guards Brigade. An Irish Guardsman commented that the pairings were formed on the basis of 'a matter of temporary convenience... who happened to be sitting in the next field.'[10] The Guards' orders for BLUECOAT were hastily re-written. Orders received by the lead units, 2/Battalion Irish Guards (tanks) and 5/Coldstream Battalion (infantry), stipulated that they should 'advance together as a battle group'. Sadly, this was the first either unit had heard of any such concept. There was chaos in the ranks as two colonels plus three hundred officers and non-commissioned officers struggled first to understand the meaning of the order and then to execute it. The Official History paints a picture of

> *'...the scrambling confusion of men, tanks and trucks, guns, carriers and motor cycles, shouting officers, desperate sergeants and patient Guardsmen.'*

Finally, order was established and alternating companies of tanks and infantry formed up on the road south of Caumont. Engines started and the column moved south.

THE IRISH-COLDSTREAM GUARDS GROUP

The Guards column struggled forward towards St-Martin-des-Besaces along a road already filled to overflowing with the 'tail' elements of 11th Armoured, 15th Scottish, and 6th Guards Tanks. Lieutenant Colonel Finlay of the 2/Irish Guards could only describe the traffic situation as 'grotesque'. Finally clear of St Martin, the column had to pass around the foot of the dominating Hill 238 [modern 226]. From the summit, elements of *21. Panzerdivision* watched their every move, and the advancing Guards were suddenly subjected to accurate artillery fire. The lead squadron of Irish Guards spurred forward. Scattering like 'a covey of partridges', they spread out to the east of the road. Sherman tanks forded the valley of the

The 'grotesque' traffic jam in St-Martin-des-Besaces.

Sherman tanks forded the stream and charged uphill. (See map on page 97)

Petite Souleuvre and, charging uphill to meet the enemy, quickly became lost in a maze of small fields. As the evening gloom descended the leading tanks formed harbour and waited for the infantry to catch up. But the Coldstream had also lost their way, reporting that they were on the tanks' position when they were in fact some distance to the west, on the summit of Hill 192 [modern 195], which they took to be 238. As night fell, the infantry pulled back a short way to the foot of the real Hill 238, where a few tanks descended to accompany them as they dug in. General O'Connor's demand that the advance be prosecuted into the hours of darkness was not heeded, and he himself did not press the matter. It had been an unpromising start. Infantry-tank co-operation would take time to achieve.

By dawn on 1 August, the Germans had disappeared from the summit of Hill 238. But the vital road winding around the base of the hill and south to le Tourneur was still covered by enemy fire. At first light, the Irish Guards' 1 Squadron and a company of Coldstream infantry moved out to secure the stretch of road crossing Point 192. These were ambushed by tanks of *21. Panzerdivision*. An entire troop of Sherman tanks was lost, and temporarily without armour support the Coldstream could make no progress. Lieutenant Colonel Adeane, commanding the Irish-Coldstream group, then prepared a set-piece attack to clear the road. But as the attack was getting under way around 10.00 hours, a mortar salvo put both Adeane and the leading infantry company commander out of action, leading to confusion and further losses. Towards the end of the morning,

The western slopes and summit of Hill 238 viewed from the road. (See map on page 97)

the brigadier arrived on the scene and ordered a halt to further advance.

THE GRENADIER GUARDS GROUP

The Grenadier group included the tanks of 2/(Armoured) Grenadier Guards and 1/(Motor Battalion) Grenadier Guards. This latter form of infantry unit deserves some explanation.

The British Army was among the first to equip its infantry battalions with motor transport. In 1944, most German infantry units were still dependent on the horse and wagon as their principal wheeled transport. By contrast, from 1938 the British set about mechanising their infantry. Whilst continuing to march on foot, every rifle platoon was to have its own 15-cwt truck to carry its equipment; and at a pinch a company commander could dump all his stores and use his four trucks to 'lift' an entire platoon. Furthermore, 'motorised battalions' were instituted: rifle battalions with a permanent allocation of Royal Army Service Corps 3-ton lorries. The rarer 'motor battalions' were most commonly found in armoured divisions, quite often with one 'motor company' detached to accompany each tank battalion. Such a company travelled into battle in armoured vehicles: typically organised into a scout platoon with up to eleven carriers, and three rifle platoons each equipped (by 1944) with an American built half-track for each squad. The motor battalions frequently augmented their firepower above the 'official' tables of organisation and equipment, scrounging extra automatic weapons wherever possible. Noel Bell of 8/Rifle Brigade recalled that his company:

> '...acquired many .50 Brownings from the 3rd R.T.R., who found them superfluous on their Shermans. We mounted them on our trucks and carriers and even on our scout car.'[11]

By the morning of 1 August, the Grenadier Guards group was positioned in and around St Martin, awaiting the call to advance in the wake of the Irish-Coldstream group. But there they were to stay throughout the day, with the sole exception of a single company ordered forward to support the Coldstream in their attempt to clear the road. The King's Company, 1/Grenadier Guards moved forward as far as Point 192. There they waited several hours until, late in the afternoon, with enemy activity appearing to slacken, they were ordered forward with a single troop of 2/Irish Guards tanks to probe the road to le Tourneur, and if possible to rush and seize the vital bridge there. This small but highly mobile group made rapid progress until brought to a halt just north of le Tourneur by a roadblock supported by two enemy tanks. The company commander Major Baker sent out infantry armed with PIATs to test the flanks of the roadblock, and eventually the enemy force moved out rather than risk being encircled. The Grenadiers then moved closer to le Tourneur and, with night approaching, crested the last hill before the small town, with the bridge beyond it in sight. Below could be seen German forces retreating through the town. At this point, Baker determined that with darkness descending, tank action would be out of the question and so attacking the town would be suicidal. The small force fell back to the north: the Irish Guards tanks to harbour with their regiment and the infantry to pass the rest of the night on a ridge line just south of Point 192.

Nevertheless, the bridge was vital to the next day's advance. In the small hours of the morning, two infantry companies of 3/Irish Guards were ordered south to the village, the companies advancing either side of the road. Two officers braved the road itself: reconnaissance officer Lieutenant Jones and Major Neale, commander of 615 Field Squadron, Royal Artillery. The infantry force had disappeared into the dark, either side of the village. Neale's scout car crept into le Tourneur, passing between burning buildings. In the large open square Neale spotted a Panzer IV, its gun pointed straight towards the road and its interior lights

The church square in le Tourneur.

glowing through open vision slits. While the car was quickly hidden in a side street, Neale reconnoitred the bridge and was delighted to find it still unblown. Returning to the car, he found Jones and the driver preparing grenades to destroy the tank. The three stalked the Panzer, finding it – like the bridge it had guarded – abandoned and intact (refurbished by 5th Guards Brigade workshops, it subsequently did sterling service as a recovery vehicle). By dawn, Le Tourneur was in British hands.

By the end of 1 August, the Guards had taken heavy losses and succeeded in putting to flight the German forces on their immediate front. But they had still not advanced across the Souleuvre to establish the link with 11th Armoured so vital to the progress of VIII Corps. As one commentator, a major with 11th Armoured, was later to record, 'A sense of urgency seems to have been lacking'.[12]

A Great War *poilu* guarding the church in le Tourneur.

Abandoned Panzer IV.

11th Armoured at the village of la Ferronnière (which they believed to be St Charles de Percy, see Appendix I, page 189). This street is now a cul-de-sac, by passed by the main road.

Coldstream Shermans pass Grenadier Churchills as they drive south into 'Mortar Gulch' (modern view on page 141). Note that the British army drives on the right in France. (See page 181.)

A captured Panzer IV of the *21. Panzerdivision* being towed away to the workshops by a Sherman recovery vehicle.

LE BENY-BOCAGE

11th Armoured Division began the day at the Souleuvre bridgehead, far to the south west of the Guards' struggle to pass Hill 238. First to move off in the pre-dawn hours were the cars of the Household Cavalry. The officer commanding D Squadron was due a rest day, but recalls:

> *'Colonel Abel Smith arrived in a cloud of dust and avalanche of maps...*
> *We, the regiment, had done "extremely well"; the corps commander was*
> *"delighted"... he announced that we were about to have the chance of doing*
> *even better within the next twelve hours.'*

The armoured cars were ordered to make their way westward to join the Torigni-Vire road and then south in the direction of Etouvy and – who knows – possibly even as far as the strategically important town of Vire. To D Squadron:

> *'Vire, even on the smallest scale map, looked very far away, especially at*
> *night.'*

The cars started their engines and, under the stars and the chains of

German tracer bullets arcing across the night sky, resumed their weary journey behind enemy lines.

By first light, the tanks were ready to move out. One more prisoner had walked into the bridgehead, confirming that the enemy ahead was *21. Panzerdivision,* but the German machine guns firing sporadic bursts through the night had by now evaporated. B Squadron went back up the hill to the south, using a narrow track discovered the previous evening. The enemy had gone from the hilltop, leaving behind in their haste a small quartermaster's store which 'caused great excitement until it was found to contain nothing of any great interest'. (Throughout the campaign, British troops were to find German field rations disappointing, although liberating wine and spirits from the Germans always remained good sport.)

The leading Hussar squadron passed Sergeant Dixon's now completely burnt-out Sherman tank and rolled on along the open road to le Bény-Bocage. As C Squadron approached the small town, the order was received to halt at a crossroads to allow a relieving regiment to pass through. Most of the tank crews were only too happy to brew tea, prepare a meal, or wash in the water of a nearby stream, while the Monmouths infantry dismounted and began clearing the farms in the area. But the leading tank of C Squadron's 3 Troop, commanded by Sergeant Sear, had continued into le Bény-Bocage. Cautiously advancing into the small town, Sear's tank was fired upon by a German Panzer IV, H or J type, and his return shot crippled the Panzer, hitting one of its tracks. The German crew managed to reverse their vehicle out of Sear's line of sight, whereupon the Panzer IV was abandoned and blown up, its debris scattered across the town square. It

La Valleé Survillé where 23/Hussars rested.

N

The Panzer IV destroyed in le Bény Bocage.

The same spot in 2002.

Sergeant Sear was mobbed by the crowd.

was the standard practice of both sides during the Normandy campaign to ensure that any immobilised tank – friendly or enemy – should be thoroughly demolished if there was a chance of its falling into enemy hands. Front line combat engineers had standing orders and equipment to achieve this, and their efficiency is attested by the total devastation of the Bény-Bocage Panzer IV.

3/Royal Tank Regiment duly arrived and passed through the town unopposed by Germans, although somewhat encumbered by the celebrations of the townspeople. Le Bény-Bocage had barely been touched by the war and the sight of British troops passing through in such numbers was enough to convince the French that their liberation was permanent. Dismounting from the 3/RTR tanks, 4/Shropshire Light Infantry were first to enjoy the celebratory mood. Later in the day, 8/Rifle Brigade moved into the place and Rifleman Kingsmill of G Company recorded in a letter home:

> 'I have never seen people so crazy with joy... A policeman at the lower end of the square hangs up an enormous tricolour flag... Everyone throws flowers and the vehicles are decorated with them. Then, not from pity but because it delights us to do so, it is our turn to give them candy... "Drunkenness", "delirium". It is difficult to find the right word... The whole village is crazy, crazy with joy.'[13]

83

The Hussars enjoyed a brief celebration in le Bény-Bocage.

Later, the Hussars were called forward and their regimental history coyly states 'we moved into the little town on a beautiful sunny afternoon to have a brief rest'. In fact, they were mobbed. Sergeant Sear had already been adopted as the local hero, photographed with the local Gendarme by the wreckage of the Panzer IV in the marketplace. Now as the regiment dispersed into yards and gardens, the townspeople were quick to show the Hussars their appreciation. Quite frequently this took the form of calvados, the local apple brandy distilled from cider, an acquired taste and widely recognized to be superior to army petrol as fuel for cigarette lighters.

3/RTR's A Squadron quickly moved out of le Bény-Bocage and, with A and D Companies of 4/KSLI accompanying, took the dominating ridge north of the town. There the two regiments' commanding officers set up their headquarters. The Shropshires pressed on still further north to secure the bridge over the Souleuvre. Unlike the heights above le Bény-Bocage, the bridge was hard-won. The Germans defended tenaciously, and the British approach was made difficult as it was limited to the steep-sided, thickly-wooded slopes leading down to the bridge. Both commanders, Colonel Silvertop of 3/RTR and Major Robinson of 4/KSLI, had to abandon their scout cars and struggle forward on foot through pine trees in order to follow the progress of the attack. The bridge was taken and B and C Companies passed through, with a squadron of tanks in support.

By taking the bridge, 4/KSLI and 3/RTR had effectively cut the road from Vire to Caen. This was a vital artery. Through what remained of the day, unsuspecting German vehicles continued to fall into ambush as they approached from both directions. When Captain Clayton of the Shropshires' B Company was injured in the fight for the bridge, a captured German staff car seemed ideal to take him to the rear, and he was bundled in. Sadly, on its way to le Bény-Bocage, the German car was fired on by British tanks outside the town and the captain wounded even more severely. The remorseful British troopers dosed the captain with morphia, but in their haste forgot to mark his forehead with the normal warning to prevent further dosing. Fortunately Clayton's constitution was strong enough to withstand both bullets and medication. Meanwhile, beyond the bridge, the KSLI were met by the sound of clapping, and advanced to find the villagers applauding their liberators. Monsieur le Maire handed over a

Steep sided wooded slopes led down to the main road.

token German prisoner. The village of Cathéolles was secured (this had been the day's ultimate objective for Guards Armoured, albeit from the north not the south!) A small party was sent ahead to the fork in the road leading to le Tourneur; here stiff opposition was encountered from German forces. The KSLI advanced no further.

GERMAN RESISTANCE

The divisions of *LXXIV Korps* were performing better than might have been expected, albeit at a heavy price. *326. Division* commanded by *Generalleutnant* Viktor von Drabich-Waechter was even putting in counter attacks and had achieved some local successes. The cost in men and equipment was considerable, including some of the *LXXIV Korps'* reserve *Jagdpanther*. It also included Drabich-Waechter himself, killed early in the battle by a devastating bombardment whilst directing an attack by *Füsilierbataillon 326*.

German defensive tactics developed from the First World War and honed in three years of bitter fighting on the Russian front proved highly effective in Normandy. The front lines – the 'Forward Edge of the Battle Area' – were thinly manned to minimize losses to opening artillery barrage. Behind this thin crust, German defensive lines were deep, absorbing the impact of assault by a numerically superior enemy, slowing his advance and buying time for reinforcements to arrive. As soon as the enemy was brought to a halt, German doctrine insisted on immediate counter attack, before the attacking force could establish itself on the objective, before it could draw breath, reorganise, and re-provision. Even remnants of outnumbered German units that had suffered severely in combat were capable of this, recovering to form *ad hoc* battlegroups which continued to perform a useful role on the battlefield. This was a function of doctrine and training.

In contrast to the British system of

Junior leaders were were encouraged to use initiative.

Schütze 1, the all-important squad machine gunner with his MG42 (refered to as the 'Spandau' by the Allies).

regimental independence, the German infantry were trained in a highly standardised manner which permitted new units to be quickly formed from companies or even squads of mixed origin. The building blocks of infantry organisation were common to all. And to avoid creative leadership being stultified by uniformity, junior leaders were encouraged to use their initiative to an extent rare in the British and virtually non-existent in the Russian armies. It was drummed into junior officers' heads that orders stood only so long as the assumptions on which they were given remained valid. Leadership meant responding to new circumstances. Even non-commissioned officers were expected to make their own decisions without waiting for confirmation from above. So, even after taking casualties, a small unit would usually have someone left ready to assume command. To this day, the German term *'Kampfgruppe'* means rather more than simply a 'battle group'; it conveys an *ad hoc* formation with a common understanding of tactics under dynamic leadership.

Furthermore, at squad level German doctrine differed fundamentally from that of the British and American armies. Instead of the rifle being the backbone of squad firepower, supported by a squad machine gun, German tactics gave the machine gun primacy. The squad – or *Gruppe* – was built around the squad machine gun. This was the MG34, later the improved and cost-reduced MG42 (collectively known by the Allies as the

'Stellung! Feuer frei!' **The MG34 team ready for action.**

'Spandau'). The MG34 had an impressive rate of fire: up to 900 rounds per minute, versus the British infantry squad's Bren gun which, for all its unquestioned accuracy, could only manage 500. Indeed, American intelligence reports suggested that the MG34 was wasteful: 'the rate of fire is probably too high for the weight'; and to the MG42's further increase in cyclic rate to 1,200 rounds per minute, the only comments were that: 'this increased rate of fire is not desirable from any point of view' and 'a certain decrease in accuracy has resulted'.[14] This entirely missed the point. Soldiers' accounts mention the considerable morale effect of the sound made by this weapon's firing (a continuous rasp, likened to a tearing bedsheet, quite unlike the stuttering sound of a Bren gun). For many new to battle, this unfamiliar yet never-

Only a boy but he already knows that in Normandy the most important items are his shovel for digging-in and ammunition to feed the voracious squad MG42.

88

forgotten sound was the first indication that the enemy was nearby. On the battlefield, the MG34 had an effective suppressive capability. Unusually for an air-cooled machine gun, the German infantry favoured long bursts of fire. One man and his assistant, liberally supplied with belts of ammunition, could keep enemy heads down over a wide area. And men with their heads below the parapets of their entrenchments were not taking part in the firefight. Consequently, the ordinary German infantryman 'Schütze' became much more an ammunition carrier than a rifleman. And as a further consequence, the *Gruppe* became extremely resilient. So long as there was someone to man the machine gun, losses of personnel would not immediately or greatly reduce the squad's firepower.

This goes some way to explaining why we so often read of major German formations being defeated, only to find their sub-units appearing and re-appearing in subsequent actions. By 31 July, the *326. Infanteriedivision* had been shattered, its positions overwhelmed, its general killed and divisional headquarters disrupted. And yet, sub-units of the division continued to resist in key areas, and were to remain in action for days to come. South of St-Martin-des-Besaces, as Guards Armoured struggled forward through almost impenetrable traffic jams, groups of infantrymen of *326 Infanteriedivision* had been hastily reassembled. Stiffened by newly-arriving armoured vehicles and *Panzergrenadiere* of *21 Panzerdivision*, men of the *326. Infanteriedivision* were forged once again into some semblance of a fighting force.

21st PANZER DIVISION

Late on Monday 31 July, *Generalmajor* Edgar Feuchtinger had been ordered to use his *21. Panzerdivision*, to support Drabich-Waechter's counter attack through the Bois du Homme and retake Hill 309. Although in contact with the enemy on many points from Dickie's Bridge to the Bois du Homme, *21. Panzerdivision* had not attacked anywhere. Furious, *LXXIV Korps* commander *General der Infanterie* Erich Straube visited Feuchtinger's battle headquarters and insisted on a morning counter-attack. Midnight found Feuchtinger back at Straube's headquarters, arguing the futility of counter-attack. It was pointless, he maintained, now that the British had broken through and crossed the Souleuvre. Only under protest and on threat of court martial did Feuchtinger agree to carry out the attack, later recalling:

> 'As I could not stop this senseless attack, I considered it more in the interest of my men to obey.'

Less than two weeks after the failed attempt by elements of the German officer corps on the life of the *Führer*, prevarication was a dangerous game for a senior *Wehrmacht* officer to play. Others took refuge in blind obedience. American General George Patton asked a captured general why he and others like him went on fighting in a hopeless cause, to be told by the German officer 'I am a professional and I obey my orders'.[15]

Feuchtinger's *21. Panzerdivision*, inherited the mantle of the division which had fought under Rommel in the desert and gained a reputation for endurance and daring. In fact, the original 21st had virtually disappeared when the desert army surrendered at Tunis in February, 1943. Feuchtinger's new division was created from scratch in May of that year, and like many new German divisions raised at that time had to scrounge and extemporise the equipment it needed to become battleworthy. The revival of such a famous name did not go unnoticed by the Allies: ULTRA decrypts allowed the Supreme Command to follow the progress of the division from Germany to Brittany and on to the Caen sector.[16] On 6 June, elements of the division guarding the Orne River and Canal bridges north of Caen had been the first German ground troops to engage Allied airborne forces on D-Day. But like the British 'Desert Rats', *21. Panzerdivision*, never quite lived up to the exalted reputation of its desert predecessors.

Confident soldiers of the élite *Hitler Jugend* Division.

Feuchtinger himself did not command the respect of all his officers, sometimes absent without leave, his slow response to the events of 6 June was rumoured to be the result of his being preoccupied that night with a lady friend. He was eventually to be relieved and court martialled. Feuchtinger, for his part, put on record his view that while the officers of *21. Panzer* reached a good standard:

'...the junior officers, NCOs, and enlisted men were not so suitable. The NCOs and enlisted men were taken from static batteries on the coast and on the Atlantic islands. They were too old, and useless for an armoured command.'[17]

Throughout the fighting around Caen, the *12. SS Panzerdivision 'Hitler Jugend'* had been highly critical of their neighbours, accusing *21. Panzer* of being unwilling to press home its attacks with the same spirit and commitment as the Hitler Youth division. The judgement was

90

Generalmajor Edgar Feuchtinger, commander of *21 Panzerdivision* inspects *Sturmgeschütz-Abteilung 200*. The general bemoaned his outdated equipment and questioned the suitability of his junior officers.

a tough one; few divisions in 1944 could stand comparison with the superbly trained *12. SS Panzer*.

In the final analysis, *21. Panzerdivision*, had been fighting since 6 June and was tired. A staff officer, *Kapitän* Eberhard Wagemann reflected that even before the invasion, 'We were conscious that neither our men nor our tanks were good enough'.

Allied intelligence estimated that *21. Panzerdivision*, might be able to oppose the landings with 'as many as 240 tanks and 40 assault guns, including a Panther battalion and possibly some Tigers'.

While the 40 assault guns were accurately reported, Feuchtinger's actual tank strength was only 127, and these were all Panzer IV. What is more, photographic evidence reveals that even of these included a number of antiquated early versions of the Panzer IV with guns and armour greatly inferior to the current models. The division was effectively starved of equipment (incidentally leading to some ingenious improvisations by Major Becker based on captured French armoured vehicles to equip the division's self-propelled gun unit, *Sturmgeschütz-Abteilung 200*). A measure of the situation is the division's tank strength on 1 August. By this date, of a total strength of 139 tanks (all various models of Panzer IV) and forty-seven turretless assault guns, only forty-two and twenty-one (respectively) were fit for action. Feuchtinger was also weak in infantry. Towards the end of July, the *16 Luftwaffedivision* (airforcemen converted to infantry for want of serviceable aircraft) had been disbanded following its heavy losses during the 'GOODWOOD' battle. Two thousand of these men were forwarded to *21 Panzerdivision*. Panzer grenadiers they were not, but they would of necessity be called upon to play their part in the planned counter attack.

In fact, an important part of the offensive capability remaining to *21 Panzerdivision* was an attached unit: *3. Kompanie* of *schwere Panzer Abteilung 503* with its complement of thirteen operational *Königstiger*. At sixty-nine tons, this 'King Tiger' was by a considerable margin the heaviest battle tank of the Second World War. It carried the same 8.8cm gun as the *Jagdpanther*, but in a fully rotating turret. Its turret front armour matched that of the *Jagdpanther* and its front hull was half as thick again. In combat, the greatest vulnerability of this massive vehicle was its running gear, but it would take a brave and extraordinarily lucky gunner to succeed in an immobilizing shot against wheels or tracks. Oddly, one of the first King Tigers to be knocked out during the Normandy campaign was lost to a British two-inch mortar. Fired by A Company, 5/Duke of Cornwall's Light Infantry, into the village of le Plessis-Grimault, a single 51mm mortar bomb chanced to hit an ammunition truck in the act of resupplying one of the 503's King Tigers.[18] There was a chain reaction and the resulting explosion

An early model *PzKw IV Ausf.C*, pulled out of a training school and sent into combat in Normandy.

Königstiger: **the Porsche turret with its distinctive curved front was more commonly found in Normandy.**

inside the tank blew out its hull roof plates and lifted the Tiger's massive turret off. This was, of course, a freak accident. More *Königstiger* in Normandy were abandoned by their crews after mechanical breakdown than were ever lost to antitank fire.[19]

FEUCHTINGER'S COUNTER ATTACK

The night of 31 July-1 August was mostly peaceful for the Scots regiments around Hill 309, 'Quarry Hill'. From 05.30 hours on 1 August, the silence was broken as precious German hordes of artillery shells, mortar bombs, and *Nebelwerfer* rockets were expended in a half-hour barrage on the hill. Shortly after dawn, *21 Panzerdivision* erupted from the Bois du Homme. Following their normal assault procedure, the Germans came forward in small groups of infantry, supported closely by armour as they attempted to infiltrate the British line. This was in sharp contrast to the linear advance generally practised by the British infantry in

The *Nebelwerfer*. Light, simple and deadly.

93

15cm rockets being loaded in to a six tube *Nbw 41*.

German infantry co-operating with armour.

Normandy. Individual German squad leaders would use their initiative to seek out dead ground, uncovered by enemy fire, occupy it, then repeat the process until in a favourable position to enfilade the British positions with flanking fire. When a weak point was identified, it was rapidly exploited and tanks brought forward to widen the gap. Particularly hard hit were 7/ Seaforth Highlanders, dug in on the lower south slopes of the hill. On this sector, the attack came in both directly from the wooded Bois du Homme and from the north east flank where the Germans exploited a gap between the defences of Hill 309 and the Royal Scots around la Ferriere-au-Doyen.

Against this classic German attack, the British responded with their own trump card: massive artillery strikes, delivered at short notice and with extreme precision. Still, between 11.00 hours and midday, the Germans' own bombardment reached a new crescendo in support of further groups of attackers. The battle raged across a six kilometre front: from les Loges where the Argylls were dug in on the lower slopes of Hill 226 across to la Mancellière, south east of St-Martin-des-Besaces. A threat was perceived to the Allied right; the vital road through St Martin had to be safeguarded. The Cameronians were ordered forward from their defence of Launay and, with support from the Coldstream Churchills and the 15th Division's reconnaissance regiment, the hamlets of Galet and la Mancellière were cleared. Then, around 16.00 hours, the fight reached a

further level of intensity as *21 Panzerdivision* – like a football team needing a goal with the last minutes ticking away – threw men and tanks forward across the battle front. Eight field regiments plus corps-level medium artillery responded with co-ordinated defensive fire. The 15th Scottish Division historian relates:

'They were met by everything we had got – medium and field artillery, 4.2 and 3 inch mortars, medium machine guns. Some were taken prisoner, some came in under a white flag, the rest broke.' [20]

Wherever they had appeared, nothing could stop the King Tigers' advance. Even the Armour Piercing Discarding Sabot ammunition, top secret until 6 June and issued now for the first time to 6th Guards Tank

The 'Mediums'. Loading a 5.5 inch gun.

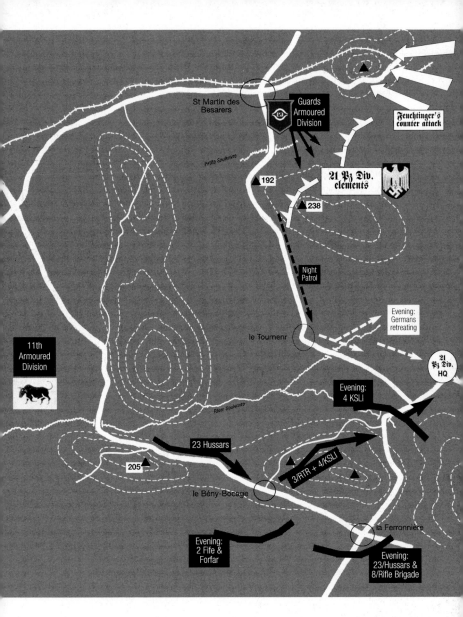

St Martin des
Besarers

Guards
Armoured
Division

Feuchtinger's
counter attack

Petite Soulenre

192

21 Pz Div.
elements

238

Night
Patrol

Evening:
Germans
retreating

le Tournenr

11th
Armoured
Division

21
Pz Div.
HQ

Evening:
4 KSLI

River Soulevre

23 Hussars

3/RTR + 4/KSLI

205

le Bény-Bocage

la Ferronniere

Evening:
2 Fife &
Forfar

Evening:
23/Hussars &
8/Rifle Brigade

Brigade's 6-pounder-armed Churchills, could no more than scratch the
frontal armour of a King Tiger. As for the 75mm-armed Churchills, as one
tank commander put it:

*'I believe there were odd spots on them where the armour was thin
enough to allow a 75 millimetre shell to penetrate, but these spots were
harder to find than a needle in any haystack I've seen.'*[21]

The best the British defenders could do was to call down artillery to hold off the tanks' accompanying infantry and – given extreme good luck – hope that a solid hit or even a near miss by a 5.5 inch 'Medium' shell might immobilize a Tiger or at least stun its crew.

The final act was played out late in the afternoon. A gap had been forced open between the Seaforth around Hill 309 and the Royal Scots on the south slopes of Hill 226, and reports were coming back of German tanks massing in the Bois du Homme. To meet this threat, 6/Kings Own Scottish Borderers were sent for. It was Minden Day, and true to tradition the colour-sergeants of the KOSB had that morning distributed roses to the men. By afternoon the flowers had wilted under the summer sun, so as the Borderers advanced into battle the riflemen – like their predecessors in 1759 – picked fresh red blooms from gardens and hedgerows to wear in the camouflage scrim nets of their helmets.[22] Attacking uphill towards the main St Martin-Villers Bocage road, the three lead companies ran into heavy mortar fire, and B Company in the centre lost their commander, Major Henson. Prisoners from the *125. Panzergrenadier Regiment* confirmed that a further major attack was in preparation, and once again the treeline of the Bois du Homme was worked-over by the British artillery. Then the rocket-firing Typhoons swept across the ridge.

An entire German battalion group had been caught as it formed up to attack. Furthest forward, the men of 6/KOSB were first to realise that the fight had gone out of the Germans. Woollcombe relates:

'We were hardened by this time to any sight. We trod on the bodies of those blond boys with hardly a thought, and I was sent on a special patrol

The British view of the dark wooded hilltop of the Bois du Homme. Down the far slope Woollcombe 'trod on the bodies of those blond boys with hardly a thought'.

N◄————

down into the woods the other side to see if there were any live ones left. There were only the dead.'[23]

Over two hundred German bodies were left behind. The war diary of *Panzergruppe* West records General Feuchtinger's report:

> *'The attack of 21 Panzerdivision did not succeed; the replacements received from the 16 Luftwaffedivision did not measure up to the demands made of them.'*

He might have added 'I told you so'. His *21 Panzerdivision* was in retreat. Already fearful that both 11th and 7th Armoured Divisions were loose in his rear (the latter a misunderstanding), Feuchtinger's apprehensions were confirmed by reports from a detached battalion of his *125. Panzergrenadier Regiment* that the enemy had secured the Bény-Bocage ridge. Suddenly, there came the news that the enemy were as far east as Cathéolles – actually, the small 3/RTR and 4/KSLI party that had halted on meeting heavy opposition. This small British force did not realise that, barely a mile further up the road, the battle headquarters of *21 Panzerdivision* had been directing holding actions against Guards Armoured and bitterly contesting Hill 309. Now fearing imminent overrun, Feuchtinger's staff fled, abandoning vehicles in their haste to escape the threat. As the day wore on, a more general collapse of the German line began as equipment, two field hospitals, and even three King Tigers were left behind in a rush to escape encirclement. This was the movement observed by the Guards patrol that had overlooked le Tourneur before retiring north for the night.

11th ARMOURED OUT ON A LIMB

During the afternoon of 31 July, 'Pip' Roberts had ventured forward with two HQ tanks through the Forêt l'Evêque to the area south of la

Ferrière-Harang. He stopped short of the bridge, conscious of how far he was from his divisional headquarters, to which he returned about 17.30 hours to find orders from O'Connor. These orders took account of the fact that VIII Corps, not XXX Corps, was now 'leading' the Operation, also of the new, more westerly axis of the advance since the capture of Dickie's Bridge. These orders indicated an advance in the direction of Vire. Roberts was to secure 'Point Aunay' road junction, where the St Martin-Villedieu road crossed the Torigni-Vire road. This lay well to the north west of the Forêt l'Evêque, and if held would be the obvious highway by which to approach Vire. As a secondary objective, Roberts was to occupy Points 204 [modern 204, two kilometres west of Dickie's Bridge], 205 [modern 207, two kilometres east of the bridge, overlooking the road to le Bény-Bocage], and 266 [modern 262, two kilometres east of le Bény-Bocage and commanding the main Vire-Villers-Bocage road].

'Pip' Roberts' dynamism had led to the Bény-Bocage ridge line being taken even before he received these written orders. As for the 'Point Aunay' road junction, we have already seen that Roberts found this in American hands. In spite of high-level agreements that this road was to be used by the British, it is understandable that the American 5th Division commander would want to use any road that assisted his advance. This was far from being an issue of nationalities; 11th Armoured had suffered equally in their move up to Caumont when Roberts noted:

> 'Certain times were given us when we would have priority on the roads,
> but in fact no one else took any notice of them.'

Delay certainly was caused as British and American troops tried to use the same road, but Roberts used 'every possible channel' to defuse a possibly awkward situation; an alternative route was proposed to the American 5th Division and then 'all was peace between us, and during the rest of the operation we never saw them again'. One suspects that Roberts' comment that he 'was quite unable to find the Pt 204 given in the order' may have been a diplomatic 'blind eye' on his part. The feature was quite clearly marked on his 1:50,000 scale map of the area, but it was a hilltop west of Dickie's bridge and well within the American sector!

Late in the day, 11th Armoured was poised to resume the advance south. Some Household Cavalry armoured cars returned declaring the main road to Vire open as far as the suburbs of the town, and with only scattered opposition remaining on the two roads leading south from le Bény-Bocage. There was little of the day left to exploit the opportunity, but Roberts had the division organise itself for an early start. 4/KSLI would continue to watch the north eastern approaches until such time as Guards Armoured made their appearance. Their partners 3/RTR ended a busy day with one squadron motoring south as far as the road junction at la Ferronnière where they supported G Company of 8/RB as the infantry cleared the small town. Enemy armour was heard approaching from the south, and the road block was further strengthened by troops of M10 tank destroyers from 75/Antitank Regiment, also an additional 8/RB mortar platoon which began firing on suspected German movement to the south. But once the Germans realised the place was in British hands, they made no further moves that night.

Infantry antitank troops and dispatch riders near Carville.

Only in the early hours of morning did vehicles approach up the highway from Vire. These were armoured cars of the Inns of Court, returning from a long range reconnaissance. Many reconnaissance soldiers felt that one of the greatest dangers of their specialist role was the return to friendly lines. They inevitably approached from the direction of the enemy, and were ever at the mercy of a nervous sentry or trigger-happy gunner. This weary night's work ended with one car detonating a No. 75 Hawkins Grenade, laid by the Rifle Brigade on the road as an antitank mine. True to form, though fortunately in this instance, the mine did little damage. Meanwhile, 23/Hussars were advised that they would be working in future with 8/RB, a new pairing but one which was to develop into a close relationship. On their right, Shermans of the 2/Fife and Forfar Yeomanry were followed by the lorry-borne Monmouths infantry as they pushed south as far as Carville. Further west still, the Northamptonshire Yeomanry would cover the divisional right flank with only a squadron of Royal Engineers sappers for infantry support.

So, at the end of an eventful day, the British were established along the entire ridgeline: from Dickie's Bridge to le Bény-Bocage and beyond, almost as far as Cathéolles. The main road between Vire and Caen was denied to the Germans. The two principal road bridges over the Souleuvre were in British hands, although the eastern of these still did not have an open road north to St-Martin-des-Besaces and Guards Armoured Division. 11th Armoured Division was now committed to an advance deep into enemy territory, even though its sole lifeline remained the single narrow bridge over the Souleuvre captured the day before. 'Pip' Roberts was about to throw his tank-infantry groups forward with open flanks, in the full knowledge that 'on both flanks there appeared to be more opposition than in front of us'. Whether this commitment would result in a breakthrough or a catastrophe, only time would tell.

Reference

1 *Military Training in the British Army: 1949-1944 From Dunkirk to D-Day*, Timothy Harrison Place, 2000, ISBN 0-7146-5037-4, p 136.

2 *With the Jocks: A Soldier's Struggle for Europe 1944-45*, Peter White, 2001, ISBN 0-7509-2721-6, p 121.

3 Roberts, p 184-185.

4 *The 4th KSLI In Normandy: June to August, 1944*, Major 'Ned' Thornburn, 1990, p 87-88.

5 23rd Hussars', p 82-83.

6 Bishop, p 60-61.

7 *The Ever Open Eye*, B D Wilson, 1998, ISBN 1-85821-532-3, p 87-90.

8 *The Story of the Guards Armoured Division 1941-1945*, Captain the Earl of Rosse and Colonel E R Hill, 1956, p 190.

9 Graham, p 133.

10 *The Micks: The Story of the Irish Guards*, Peter Verney, 1970, ISBN 0-330-23632-6, p169-170.

11 *From the Beaches to the Baltic The Story of G Company 8th Battalion the Rifle Brigade During the Campaign in North West Europe*, Noel Bell, 1947, p 11.

12 *Normandy: The British Breakout*, J J How, 1981, ISBN 0-7183-0118-8, p 79.

13 Bell, p 33-34.

14 German Infantry Weapons, US Military Intelligence Service Special Series No. 14, May 1943.

15 Bradley, p 357.

16 Bennett, p 57-59.

17 War Crimes Trials Debriefing Document B-441, included in Fighting the Invasion: The German Army at D-Day, ed. David C Isby, 2000, ISBN 1-85367-427-3, p 114-115.

18 Taylor, p 70; *The Duke of Cornwall's Light Infantry 1939-45*, Major E G Godfrey and Major General R F K Goldsmith, 1966, p 257.

19 *Germany's Tiger Tanks: Combat Tactics*, Thomas L Jentz, 1997, ISBN 0-7643-0225-6, p 110-113; Raising Churchill's Army, David French, 2000, ISBN 0-19-820641-0, p 105.

20 Martin, p 91.

21 Mailed Fist, John Foley, 1975, ISBN 30118-037245176, p 79.

22 *Borderers in Battle*, Captain Hugh Gunning, 1948, p 111.

23 Woollcombe, p 103.

CHAPTER SIX

Wednesday 2 August –
THRUST AND COUNTER THRUST

THE DAY

This was a day of risks taken and opportunities lost. On this day, *Panzergruppe West* recognised the danger of the German defensive line in Normandy becoming fatally unhinged, and invested heavily in attempts to restore a fractured front. On the British side, initiative and daring led to a day of fluid activity quite uncharacteristic of 21st Army Group's conduct of the campaign in Normandy.

General der Panzertruppen Heinrich Eberbach.

In order to tell the story of this single day, a number of key tactical episodes have been selected as jigsaw pieces interlocking to form a wider picture. It should be understood that, on the day, no one person was in a position to see more than a fraction of this big picture. Events were determined not by generals but by company- and squadron-level actions. There were no clearly demarcated front lines. On both sides, only the forward troops really knew where the enemy was. Eberbach could only despatch his Panzer divisions into the disputed area and rely on their initiative to stabilize a confused situation. Montgomery for once lost his tight grip on developments; in the course of the day his main contribution was to deny VIII Corps an opportunity to shorten the war in France.

II SS PANZER KORPS

The maps of the German high command still showed the front line to be somewhere between Caumont and St-Martin-des-Besaces. Nevertheless, right up to the level of the army group commander, it was clear that a crisis was developing south of the Souleuvre around le Bény-Bocage. *21. Panzerdivision* had failed to hold the line. Though the full calamity of that failure was not yet realised, it was clear that more force had to be found to fill the gap. By now, *Panzergruppe West* was used to juggling the forces available, balancing the needs of sectors at lesser risk against those where certain disaster appeared imminent. In the knowledge that the British armoured divisions had moved west from Caen to Caumont, German armour could likewise be moved west.

As early as 15.00 hours on 1 August, General Heinrich Eberbach

Hohenstauffen
9th SS Panzer Division

Frundsberg
10th SS Panzer Division

Hitler Jugend
12th SS Panzer Division

forwarded von Kluge's order that *10 SS Panzerdivision 'Frundsberg'* be prepared to move from the Orne River sector to the left wing of *Panzergruppe West*. At 15.25 hours, *Frundsberg* was given its marching orders. Kluge and Eberbach debated whether more force might be required, considering the possibility of moving the veteran *12 SS Panzerdivision 'Hitler Jugend'* as well. By 16.05 hours the decision was made: *9 SS Panzerdivision 'Hohenstaufen'* would accompany its sister division to the breakthrough area. This was easier said than done. Elements of *Hohenstaufen* were still engaged in a hot fight for the ruins of Saint Martin on the Orne, where a Canadian breakthrough on a 150 metre front was being bloodily opposed. Nevertheless, the division began at once to disengage, and to its credit had its lead elements ready to roll by 17.25 hours that evening. Despite some confusion the bulk of the division was on the road west by 22.00 hours. To *Obergruppenführer* Wilhelm Bittrich's *II SS Panzer Korps* was added the command of what was left of *21. Panzerdivision*. Bittrich's orders were to shore up the breach between *LXXIV Korps'* crumbling left flank and Meindl's parachute corps on the right of *Seventh Army*.

SS-*Obergruppenführer* Wilhelm Bittrich

These movements alone justified the original Operation BLUECOAT plan. *II SS Panzer Korps* had experienced severe losses since its introduction to the Normandy battlefield in late June, but the corps remained the single most powerful armoured formation in Normandy. Hitler himself is recorded as musing that had the *Frundsberg* and *Hohenstaufen* divisions been present in Normandy on 6 June, the invasion would have been stopped in its tracks. In itself, this comment is not terribly helpful, and invites the question why these units were not present (they had been sent to the Eastern Front on Hitler's orders). Their hurried return from fighting the Russians in Galicia at the end of June was intended to be the final 'gathering of the clans' prior to a strategic counterblow designed to punch a corridor through the British lines and back to the beaches. Correspondingly, the crowning achievement of the Allies' defensive battles around Caen had been to anchor Army Group B's key strategic strike force in front line defensive positions. Now, at the beginning of August, Hitler was again pondering a strategic move to the beaches, this time to cut off the American breakthrough by sending Hausser's *Seventh Army* on an armoured drive westwards. Ironically, General of the *Waffen* SS Paul 'Papa' Hausser had earlier commanded *II Panzer Korps* on its return to Normandy. Just as he was readying his corps to lead the planned June counter offensive, *Generaloberst* Friedrich Dollmann of *Seventh Army* committed suicide and Hausser was promoted into his place. Now, desperate to reinforce *Seventh Army* and preserve the German left, Hausser was to be denied his former divisions while they attended to the British threat.

Generaloberst Friedrich Dollmann 'scapegoat' for failure to prevent Normandy landings.

THE ROAD TO VIRE

'Pip' Roberts well knew that 'August 2 was going to be an exciting day'. As he completed the preparations for the day's advance, he received news. 11th Armoured Division was denied permission to enter the town of Vire, which was declared to be in the American sector. Roberts records:

> *'This was in some ways frustrating; Vire was a very important road centre and its occupation by us would have made life very difficult for the Germans.'*

This understatement skates over a number of issues.

There can be no doubt that General O'Connor's orders of 1 August were framed with a view to an advance on Vire. British seizure of that town on 2 August was possible and would have changed the outcome of the battle for Normandy. The loss of Vire would have demanded an urgent and violent response, as the Germans' lines of supply, of reinforcement, and indeed of possible retreat for all German forces west of Vire, would be jeopardised. A German failure to re-take the town might well have precipitated a dramatic collapse of the *Seventh Army*. Whether Hitler's cherished Mortain counter offensive could have gone ahead is conjectural. What is certain is that the future of the German *Seventh Army* briefly hung in the balance.

Why Montgomery made such a curious decision has been the subject of extensive debate, and will be reviewed at the end of this narrative. But it was not for 'Pip' Roberts to reason why. Now, in the early hours of 2 August, 11th Armoured set off bound not south for Vire, but south east into the German rear. The only elements of 11th Armoured to approach Vire on 2 August were the squadrons of the Northamptonshire Yeomanry.

The Cromwell tanks of 2/Northants Yeomanry set out at first light to cover the right flank of the advancing division, lacking adequate infantry support but using their mobility as a shield while probing for German

The Northants Yeomanry set off on the road to Vire.

resistance. A and B Squadrons patrolled the main Vire highway while C Squadron ventured further west as far as Etouvy on the Vire-Torigni road. Here, C Squadron found enemy positions which they could not dislodge without infantry, and so decided to return east to la Bistière, just five kilometres north of Vire. The temptation to press on was irresistible. All the more so when excited French civilians declared that the Germans had moved out of Vire. C Squadron encountered a typical German road block at the important road junction of la Papillonière, where they knocked out a German antitank gun. Then, as was becoming commonplace in the confusion, C Squadron went on to destroy a convoy of soft-skinned vehicles that unwittingly rolled through the village. Pressing on through the outskirts of Vire, C Squadron sent two troops forward. These came under artillery fire. Vire was not entirely evacuated. By now low on ammunition, the Northants Yeomanry Cromwells regrouped and resupplied around la Papillonière.

THE HORNS OF THE BLACK BULL

It is said in the British Army that battles always take place on a hillside, in the rain, at a place where three maps overlap. At least today there was to be no rain. This was small consolation for the units chosen to be the spearhead of 11th Armoured Division. The tank crews of 23/Hussars were roused at 03.30 hours to undergo 'a great deal of fumbling because our next day's advance is to take us on to three different map sheets'.[1] The new direction of 11th Armoured Division was assisted by neither roads nor terrain. The only major highways in the sector both led out of Vire: one towards the north east (Codenamed 'COVENTRY', the N177 [modern D577], already blocked by the British between la Ferronnière and Cathéolles); and one due east ('RUGBY', the N812 [modern D512]). A third, smaller road ('WARWICK', the GC55 [modern D55]) bisected the two, running north east from Vire to Estry. With the bulk of the division now committed to an advance to the south east, the only roads available were relatively minor country lanes. And lying at right angles to the divisional advance were major whaleback ridges.

Operation BLUECOAT took place in an area of France characterised by high ridges generally running from east to west. Highest among these is the massif culminating east of St-Martin-des-Besaces with the Bois du Homme, 360m at its summit. Next in line, seven kilometres south, is the Bèny-Bocage ridge, running right across the BLUECOAT sector, its many summits reaching 200m and above, with only one significant and extremely narrow gap where the Souleuvre river cuts through the ridge line, down through 'mortar gulch' to Cathéolles, then winding on westward past Dickie's Bridge to join the River Vire. Another five or six kilometres south there begins a series of close-packed ridges, with summits running east to west reaching between 200 and 240m. The crest line of the first of these is roughly indicated by the line of the D55 road (WARWICK), passing north of Burcy and Presles and on to Estry. Barely a mile south, the Perrier ridge is less regular, its highest point being the spur topped by the two Perriers (Bas and Haut) and Chênedollé. And finally, the D512 highway leading straight-as-a-die due east out of Vire follows the 200m contour, rarely descending below 180m.

The two brigade groups leading the breakthrough were charged with crossing this terrain to reach their assigned objectives. On the left of the division, the 23/Hussars – 8/RB group was to follow the line: le Désert, Presles, Chênedollé. On its right, the 2/Fife and Forfar – 3/Monmouths group had to find a way from le Reculey to the Burcy ridge, and on to cut the Vire-Vassy road at Viessoix. From Cathéolles and la Ferronnière, 3/RTR and 4/KSLI were hoping to be relieved by Guards Armoured Division before following the lead columns, their role to head south east behind the 23/Hussars – 8RB group, to screen the division's open left flank. On the extreme right flank, 2/Northants would cover the approaches to Vire, probing the main roads through Étouvy and le Reculey towards Vire itself.

Accompanying or following closely behind these leading groups came the whole mobile panoply of the 1944 armoured division, among it the artillery. 11th Armoured's own 75/Antitank Regiment was equipped with forty-eight powerful 17-pounder antitank guns. Two of the four batteries were towed and two used the M10, a tank destroyer with an open-topped turret on a Sherman-type chassis. The division's two field artillery

An M10 self propelled 17-pounder antitank gun.

regiments each had twenty-four 25-pounder field guns: 151/Field Regiment, the Ayrshire Yeomanry, towed behind their Quads and generally working with 159 Brigade group; and 13/Royal Horse Artillery with their Sexton self-propelled guns on Canadian Ram tank chassis, generally supporting 29 Brigade group.

Towed 25-pounder guns of a Royal Artillery field regiment.

11th ARMOURED: HUSSARS AND RIFLES

At first, the 23/Hussars – 8/RB group made slow progress as small groups of Germans fought mobile holding actions. Typically, a knot of enemy infantry would form around an antitank gun or mobile tank destroyer covering a road junction or village. These would force the leading British tanks to deploy off-road, the infantry to unload and advance to contact. Then the defenders would melt away as best they could, displacing back to the next stop line. On occasion, German reconnaissance units were encountered, as in the little hamlet of la Tihardière, where a detachment of two German half-tracks was encountered trying to escape. Both were quickly destroyed by Sergeant Williams' tank at the head of B Squadron, 23/Hussars. (These were small, turreted half-tracks, model *SdKfz250/9* from *2 Kompanie* of SS-*Hauptsturmführer* Gräbner's *SS-Pz.Aufk.Abt.9*, and represented the Hussars' first encounter on this battlefield with units of *'Hohenstaufen'*). As 23/Hussars crossed the main Vire road, a German tank was reported spotted and there ensued 'a lot of excitement' before it disappeared. Crossing the highway, with no major road to follow, the Hussars'

The two *SdKfz 250/9* (one on the road, one in the field), knocked out by 23/Hussars.

The crossroads at Point 218.

commander Lieutenant Colonel Harding deployed his squadrons on a broad front, the Rifle Brigade platoons in their half-tracks and carriers following closely. The column pressed on across country.

Reaching the D55 road at Point 218 [modern 221], some infantry opposition was encountered. Here, while Sergeant Jones' B Squadron tank was dealing with *Panzerfaust*-carrying defenders, the Commanding Officer's operator chose an awkward moment to come on air with a 'netting' call. Jones patiently endured the routine of tuning and reporting signals while trying to issue fire and movement orders to his crew. At length his patience snapped and with a 'For God's sake give me more time!' he went off air to concentrate on the Germans. Later, on the same

The parallel route of the Fife and Forfars, from Point 218.

2nd Fife & Forfars line of advance

N

The D55, Objective 'Warwick'. The Panther tank brought down a telegraph pole over a Sherman.

spot, as B Squadron rolled on down into Presles and the crossroads was occupied by regimental headquarters, an artillery Forward Observation Officer began briskly firing his Sherman tank's main gun at some tanks a mile to the west. Major Blacker of the Hussars jumped down from his own Sherman and marched across. Before a medium artillery battery far to the rear could register the tempting target and pour in its 5.5inch shells, Blacker pointed out to the embarrassed FOO that his target was actually a column of 2/Fife and Forfar Shermans, advancing on a parallel course. Returning to his own tank, Blacker then perceived a real enemy in the opposite direction. A German tank was advancing westwards out of Estry, coming straight down the D55 from the north east and now barely a hundred metres away. (The enemy was identified as a mark V Panzer, a 'Panther', but it should be noted that every enemy tank spotted by the Hussars that day was likewise recorded as a 'Panther'; even at this stage of the war tank recognition was not good.) The German began firing, spraying machine gun bullets and bringing down a telegraph pole across one of the Hussars' Shermans. A great deal of confusion ensued before a Sherman tank was able to work its way around the flank of the enemy tank and destroy it. (As the enemy actually was a Panther, this was prudent. The only practical way for a Sherman's 75mm gun to penetrate a Panther was with a flank or rear shot; once their relatively thin side armour was penetrated, Panther tanks had a tendency to blow up instantly.) More trouble was encountered in Presles itself, where a German assault gun was knocked out and another found abandoned. Following the tanks into Presles, the motor infantry of 8/RB engaged Panzer grenadiers just north of the village. G Company took a prisoner, recalled by Noel Bell as: 'one of the most enormous blond Aryans I have ever seen.'[2] The Rifle Brigade treated the Panzer grenadiers to a hail of mortar bombs and moved into Presles. Sensing the presence nearby of further enemies, the Hussars and

111

Rifle Brigade were pleased to continue south, leaving Presles for somebody else to deal with.

With an open left flank, and aware of German forces lurking in that direction, the Hussars' Colonel Harding pushed A Squadron – without its RB infantry company – out to the west of the main column as a left flank guard. The rest of the column was just climbing up towards le Bas Perrier when heavy firing was heard to the north. Disaster had befallen A Squadron. Lacking infantry, it had fallen into a trap while climbing out of the little hamlet of les Moulins. Hidden in a cornfield, a number of enemy tanks had sprung their ambush at close range. The British tanks were caught in the open as they emerged from a sunken road, struck before they could shake out from close formation and subjected to converging fire from different directions. With well distributed fire the German volleys quickly destroyed all but four of A Squadron's tanks.

A key element of tanks' fire discipline is the distribution of fire: ensuring that everybody does not fire at the same target; instead spreading the fire to ensure the greatest number of kills before the element of surprise is lost. In testament to the fire discipline of the Panzers, many British accounts of Normandy tank actions begin with the sudden loss of a

The road down from Point 218 into Presles in 1944. Opposite: the same spot in 2002.

A Stuart light reconnaissance tank leads a column of Shermans across country.

number of tanks.[3] This was no exception. With a dozen tanks burning and the major of the squadron badly wounded (though still trying with more bravery than sense to resume command), Captain Geoffrey Taylor gained control of the situation. Leading the four surviving tanks back to cover, he then returned to gather up the wounded and keep the remnants of A Squadron together. Gradually, the survivors of A Squadron limped back to the main body of the Regiment. The Hussars' Reconnaissance Troop assisted, their Stuart light tanks busily clearing a path through Panzer grenadiers while the four surviving Shermans acted as a rearguard.

B Squadron had meanwhile run into its own trouble while entering the

113

Tiger tank

Entering Chênedollé.

little village of Chênedollé. One officer, Lieutenant Geoffrey Bishop, recalled:

> 'The villagers seemed to have some premonition of the horror that was to befall their little community during the next seven days, for they appeared quiet and apprehensive as the leading tank appeared.'[4]

These villagers had started the day far behind the fighting and were totally unprepared for the war to come to them. Hitherto, the advancing British had noticed a pattern: if there were civilians in sight and flags out, all was well; if the streets were empty, if the only movements were curtains twitching and the odd stray dog, then like as not trouble was waiting. In Chênedollé the pattern was broken. With the village folk still watching, a crack and a whistle heralded an antitank round cutting through the air. With a thump and a flash, Sergeant Allsopp's tank was knocked out, fortunately with little harm done to the crew beyond their pride. An officer observed Allsopp leading his crew back from their wrecked Sherman 'looking rather irritated, like someone whose car has broken down at a tiresome moment'. Carrier-borne infantry jumped out of their vehicles and, moving stealthily from building to building, began to clear the village.

Tank-infantry combat had been revolutionised in 1942 with the development of hand-held antitank weapons. An American Colonel Skinner, fascinated since boyhood with rockets, had long since been interested in the idea of a shoulder-launched rocket, but the Ordnance

Corps favoured devices that used the Springfield rifle as a grenade launcher (possibly because they saw in it a way of reducing their stockpiles of redundant M10 grenades; there was little other reason to favour the unsatisfactory rifle-mounted grenade launcher). Only with the development of the hollow-charge principle, enabling low velocity projectiles to penetrate armour, was a satisfactory projectile found for Skinner's launcher. The marrying of the two ideas produced the 'bazooka' (a cumbersome tube, named after a trombone played by a comedian of the day, Bob Burns). The device was hurried to North Africa where, in an early combat trial, a German tank detachment surrendered outright after a few rockets were launched at extreme range. The Americans were impressed. So were the Russians, who received several hundred of the first batch of bazookas produced. And so too were the Germans who promptly captured a number from the Russians and just as promptly designed a far superior version of their own. Meanwhile, the British had gone their own way with the hollow charge, and issued their infantry with a weapon the like of which has not been seen since. In a departure from normal practice, the 'Projector, Infantry, Anti-Tank' was not named after its inventor, Millis Jefferis, but as a result of War Office spite was given the unglamorous name

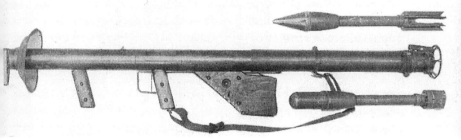

An early model American Bazooka.

German *Raketenpanzerbüchse*. Alternatively known as *Panzerschreck* (tank terror) or *Ofenrohr* (stovepipe), its 8.8cm projectile could penetrate any Allied armour.

The PIAT. We shall not see its like again.

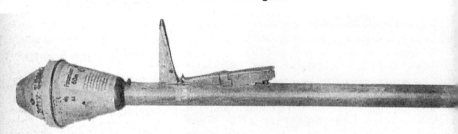

The *Panzerfaust* (armour fist). This one-man antitank weapon lacked accuracy, safety and range. But it was cheap, disposable, and potentially devastating.

The *Panzerschreck* in action.

of 'PIAT'. And unglamorous it was. Its 200-pound tension spring loosed a hollow-charge bomb which wobbled through the air for a hundred yards or more, on a good day. Of course, in open country it was not easy to 'stalk' an enemy tank to within a hundred yards, and poor aim or a dud bomb would bring fast retribution from the tank. In more built-up terrain, the PIAT team had a better chance of closing to effective firing range.

PIAT gangs worked their way into the village.

In Chênedollé on that hot and still August afternoon, silence fell as villagers disappeared indoors and the Rifle Brigade moved into the village. 'PIAT gangs' picked their way from house to house in search of the German tank that had despatched Sergeant Allsopp's Sherman. Stone buildings covered their advance, and the enemy tank was soon found, sitting menacingly in the middle of the deserted street. Hussars and Rifle Brigade accounts are consistent in referring to it as a 'Panther', as with earlier sightings. In fact, this was a Tiger tank of *s.SS-Pz.Abt. 102*, of which we shall hear more later. But whether Panther or Tiger, the PIAT gangs faced a formidable adversary. The tension broke with a violent explosion against the tank's turret. Smoke plumed upwards. A second PIAT bomb flew, and again a solid hit was registered on the turret. To the firers' dismay, the tank was not penetrated. The tank lurched forward, crashed to a halt,

117

then engaging reverse gear it ground away backwards, disappearing around a building. The PIAT teams were relieved to have driven off the monster, though annoyed that it could have survived two direct hits which they felt should have reduced the turret crew 'to porridge'. To the credit of the infantry, the tank's turret crew were quite likely injured by flying metal inside the fighting compartment (as experienced German tank crews well knew, even fragments of paint sent flying from turret walls could inflict unpleasant wounds), or at least stunned by the blasts. Nevertheless, by the PIAT teams' efforts, Chênedollé had briefly been secured.

Late in the afternoon, the Hussar and Rifle Brigade commanders took stock of the situation. They had achieved the day's objective. Their right appeared secure; the Fife and Forfars had just reported that they were on the Vire-Vassy road. But to the south and the east lay enemy territory, in all probability crawling with enemy tanks. The position seemed very insecure, with little or no room to manoeuvre on the narrow hilltop. A decision was made. The entire group would pull back a mile to the north to take up positions for the night on the broader heights around the village of le Bas Perrier. As darkness fell, the remnants of A Squadron came into the perimeter, and the Hussars and Rifles group went into close leaguer in the fields.

11th ARMOURED: FIFES AND MONMOUTHS

2/Fife and Forfarshire Yeomanry were awoken at first light. Lieutenant Steel Brownlie and his crew had slept under their Sherman tank. At the end of a gruelling day, they had harboured on a steep grassy slope of the Bény-Bocage ridge. After completing the chores of refitting, rearming, and refuelling, the exhausted crew crept between the tracks of the tank to sleep. This was no place for the claustrophobic, as the tank cleared the ground by barely eighteen inches. No one liked the idea of being crushed, least of all by their own tank, but the ground seemed firm enough. All the crew were somewhat alarmed on waking to find their sheltering Sherman tank had slithered a short distance sideways during the night. One more danger to add to the perils of armoured warfare.

The Fife and Forfar mounted up and advanced their tanks from Carville to le Reculey. Like the 23/Hussars, the Fifes ran into a detachment of German reconnaissance half-tracks, one of which was too slow to escape the Stuart light tanks of the Fifes' own recce troop. In the lead was Steel Brownlie, who in five weeks of fighting had moved from junior troop leader to the most senior in A Squadron, as officers became casualties. With A Squadron once again in the lead, Steel Brownlie as the most experienced troop leader led the way, and was first to inspect the German half-track, noting that there was blood about and loose sheets of paper, also a pair of periscopic binoculars which he took for his own use. The tanks rolled on,

French farmers turned out to offer guidance.

reaching the main Vire – Caen highway (Objective COVENTRY). Here a patrol of the ubiquitous Household Cavalry reported the enemy present in considerable numbers just 800 metres to the south. The cost of this information had been one of their cars knocked out by a German tank. A Squadron took up a position astride the main road while the rest of the column crossed behind the defensive screen. Later, with support from infantry of the 1/Herefordshire Regiment, A Squadron moved against the enemy, who proved to be a mixed force of tanks and infantry. Surprised and disorganised, these Germans were in no mood for a fight and soon pulled back. They were not pursued; the tanks had to continue towards their objectives in the south east. A Squadron rejoined the main body and together the column pressed on. Once across the COVENTRY highway, the

Vassy   Vire

N

The 'Rugby' road from the Perrier Ridge.

pace quickened. Not only was the terrain more forgiving, but also there was help from an unexpected quarter. French farmers, observing the Germans laying mines in the half-light of dawn, had crept out after the Germans left and placed pieces of white paper to mark each one. Steel Brownlie reflected that the tanks were able to resume 'baffing': driving flat out so as to deny any lurking enemy the time to take careful aim; firing on the move at any likely target, not so much in hopes of hitting anything, but more to keep enemy heads down until the tanks were well past.

Around midday, the head of the column crossed the D55 road (Objective WARWICK) and reached the crest of the ridgeline. The troop halted to take in a breathtaking view of lush, rolling countryside shimmering under the high summer sun. Nestled below in the valley was the little village of Burcy, the regiment's next goal. In sight to the south, some three kilometres away, was the Vire – Vassy road (Objective RUGBY), the final objective of the day. As other elements of the column crossed the ridge and descended into Burcy, movement and smoke were observed at a dark wood on a hill to the south. This was a cue for the artillery. Like the tanks, the artillery had been making the most of the easy terrain. The Ayrshire Yeomanry spent the morning leap-frogging from one firing position to another, alternately unhooking their 25-pounder field guns from their towing Quads, emplacing the guns, and preparing fire plans. In this way, while keeping up with the rapid advance of the tanks and lorried infantry, the regiment ensured that at any given time one of its three eight-gun batteries would be 'on the ground' and ready to engage a snap target. With the tanks was forward observer Captain R G V Nicoll, and no sooner was the suspicious wood to the south of Burcy identified than Nicoll was in contact with the Ayrshire Yeomanry's 124 Battery. The eight field guns quickly ranged-in and all present on the ridge above Burcy had the satisfaction of seeing enormous explosions as an enemy ammunition dump blew up.

As the bells of Burcy began to ring in joyous celebration, the last leg of the day's advance took place. Still leading the regiment, A Squadron pressed on, skirting around the German presence at 'Dump Wood' by taking a minor road running south east from Burcy. (This precaution may have been unnecessary; when the villagers from Burcy searched the wreckage of the dump in the woods around the Château le Croisel, they found no Germans remaining there.) The Squadron halted in the hilltop hamlet of Pavée. Through his newly-acquired binoculars, Steel Brownlie enjoyed a panoramic view of the 'Rugby' objective and could clearly see the Vire-Vassy road busy with German traffic running in both directions along the vital artery.

Steel Brownlie's troop of four tanks was ordered to go on ahead of the main body, to block the road until more force could be brought up. This was no time for 'baffing', as the enemy was so close. Half way from Pavée to the objective, the country lane ended at a junction with the Chênedollé road [modern Point 189], and the tanks pressed on down a dirt track, crossing the Pouraison stream then climbing up a narrow sunken way. At one point, Steel Brownlie's Sherman tank could only inch forward with one track following a rut on the ground and the other up on the bank, leaving the tank precariously balanced at a forty-five degree angle. At this point, the second in the column became stuck fast, probably sinking to its belly in the earth churned up by the lead tank. A short distance from the road, Steel Brownlie halted his tank and continued alone, putting on the German helmet he carried for such occasions and slinging his German rifle on his

The Sherman tanks pressed on down a dirt track. N

Shermans tight in a lane in the bocage.

back. And so it was that the entire VIII Corps advance south was spearheaded by a single junior officer advancing up a dirt track. For his part, Steel Brownlie was less concerned at reaching the Corps objective than he was relieved at emerging onto the pavée to find the road completely clear as far as the eye could see.

The lone officer called up his own tank, which he backed into a lane on the south side of the road, covering the eastern approach. Steel Brownlie's troop corporal then brought up his tank, which was parked on the north side, facing west. A German motorcycle approached from Vire, its unsuspecting rider slowing to wave at the officer and corporal at the roadside. Both fired, the officer with his German rifle and the corporal

The second tank became stuck fast.

with his pistol; and both hit, each putting a bullet through one of the rider's legs. (It should be noted that wounding an enemy with a pistol was a rare event; one combat medic recorded that of all the pistol wounds he treated during the war, most were self-inflicted, and most of those accidental!) The man was an *Oberfeldwebel* of *116. Panzerdivision*. He

Emerging from the track to the right, the troop corporal brought up his own tank to cover the western approaches.

Emerging from the track to the left Steel Brownlie's tank backed into a lane to cover the eastern approaches.

was dosed with morphia and laid in a ditch.

At length, the rest of A Squadron's tanks arrived on the road, and formed a defensive ring. The crews felt very exposed, though Steel Brownlie later reflected:

> *'If we had known then what was later revealed about German counter measures, we would have felt even worse.'*[5]

A column of German ambulances arrived from Vire; they were driven out of sight and their occupants joined the motorcyclist in the ditch. C Squadron arrived and further strengthened the little perimeter. Later, German tanks were observed far to the west. Before long, these began sending shots down the road, and succeeded in 'brewing up' one of the Shermans. The Germans were far beyond the effective range of the Shermans' 75mm guns, but the Ayrshire Yeomanry forward observer present was able to range the target and call for tactical air support (codenamed 'Limejuice'). The Typhoon fighter-bombers could arrive within twenty minutes from forward airstrips, and even sooner if they were already in the air, on-call in a 'taxi rank' holding pattern. As the 'tiffies' neared the scene, the observer called his distant 25-pounder battery to put red smoke down on the target, which the aircraft then pounded with salvoes of 60-pound rockets. These effectively cleared the road. Less satisfactory was the arrival of American Thunderbolt aircraft which strafed the British position for a good ten minutes. Fortunately, these fired only cannon, not rockets. The only harm done was to the German motorcyclist, who was killed, a damaged half-track, and a radio operator who cut his hand on an empty 'Compo' ration tin when he dived into a slit trench. The tank men grew fatigued under the hot sun. Trusting to assurances that his squadron would be withdrawn at nightfall, Steel Brownlie risked taking a benzedrine tablet, supposed to keep you alert for six hours, after which you collapsed. The day dragged on.

Much later, as Steel Brownlie's benzedrine pill was wearing off, his squadron was finally recalled. Recognising that the exposed position on the Vire road was not adequately defensible, the Fifes harboured along with the 3/Monmouths infantry on the Presles ridge to the north. But still, someone had to be left on the road to ensure that no Germans should sneak past into Vire under cover of darkness. This task was given to 'Codesign Steel' whose troop was to remain in place. Steel Brownlie protested in vain. All his protests achieved was the support of a 'platoon' of 3/Monmouths (which turned out to consist of a Canadian lieutenant and about fifteen men). The rest of A Squadron departed. By evening on 2 August, German forces were aggressively patrolling westward. Steel Brownlie records that it was 'no comfort to us' that the departing squadron ran into trouble on its short journey north, but it was a sharp reminder of the increasingly

A Typhoon fighter-bomber comes in to land over a supply column.

confused situation of the battlefield. A Squadron's rearmost tank was brewed up (with two dead, and three taken prisoner) while the Squadron ARV (armoured recovery vehicle – a converted Sherman tank) had to fight its way clear of an orchard where it was engaged by a German half-track.

'Codesign Steel' formed an all-round defence. Barbed wire and Hawkins grenades were strung across the road, the tank guns pointed to cover all directions. Infantry and tank crews alike were forbidden to smoke and threatened that anyone found asleep would be shot. Steel Brownlie sat disconsolately through the night, pricking his hands with pins to stay awake, and listening to a constant rumble of tracked vehicles moving some way to the south.

11th ARMOURED: ROYAL TANKS AND SHROPSHIRES

By the time Guards Armoured Division prepared to cross the le Tourneur bridge over the Souleuvre, the 11th Armoured roadblock had already departed. As dawn broke, the outposts of C Company, 4/King's Shropshire Light Infantry, holding the road junction north of Cathéolles, had heard the unmistakable sound of armoured vehicles approaching form the north. Mike Sayer, a C Company platoon commander, recalled:

'We were alarmed. If it was the Guards Armoured Division they probably would not have known Cathéolles was in Allied hands and would have shot us up. If it was the Germans we would have been in an even more unenviable position.'

The matter was not put to the test. To everyone's great relief, the outposts were called back to the bridge as the regiment prepared to move out. Guards Armoured would have to make their own way through Cathéolles.

As the morning progressed, the lorried infantry of 4/KSLI was formed up and along with 3/RTR's tanks motored south, following the route of the 23/Hussars – 8/Rifle Brigade group. It quickly became evident that, although well behind the leading units, the 3/RTR – 4/KSLI group was not exactly 'behind the lines'. The leading tanks and Lieutenant Mullock's B Company of the Shropshires had numerous encounters with the enemy, including – ominously – tanks and Panzer grenadiers of 9 *SS-Panzerdivision* Late in the day, the combined force halted just north east of the Point 218 crossroads above Presles, where 23/Hussars had earlier rebuffed the lone Panther. The tanks harboured around a small orchard and the infantry shortly joined them. Assuming that enemy attacks would come from the south, it seemed a good reverse-slope position.

The Shropshires' commander was uneasy about his left flank. He was conscious that his position was the extreme left flank of the division. He knew that the Shermans of 3/RTR would be of limited usefulness in the night, even when refuelled and rearmed. And now he was informed that Guards Armoured Division was in difficulties to the north. Before the light failed, he wanted to establish an outpost to the east. Major Thornburn's D Company was chosen to move a mile eastwards up the Estry road (along which 23/Hussars had earlier chased their lone 'Panther'), to occupy a hilltop farm at les Grands Bonfaits. D Company moved out about 20.30 hours, just as the light was beginning to fail. The company was advancing over open fields, with supporting 3/RTR tanks just visible on a parallel course some way to the north, when enemy tanks were spotted. Three Panther tanks were milling around just 400 metres away, directly to the east. 'Ned' Thornburn later related, 'I have rarely felt so helpless to avert a catastrophe'. Thornburn's wireless operator had a No. 38 Wireless Telephone, but the tanks were a half mile away, and the set's nominal three-quarter mile range was rarely achieved in practice. However, contrary to all expectations, the operator succeeded in contacting the Sherman squadron.

> 'It was almost the only occasion I can remember of a 38 set communicating with anything, but it certainly saved the whole operation on this occasion!'

The leading Sherman turned ninety degrees and led its column into the D Company area, to everyone's enormous relief. But one man was not satisfied.

As Thornburn supervised the company's establishment on the hilltop objective, Company Sergeant Major Harrison set off on a Panther hunt. Carrying the 18 Platoon PIAT, he located one of the Panthers on the road to the east, and determined to stalk the beast. Creeping to effective range, he loosed a bomb which hit the Panther's sloping front armour with a dull clang, and bounced harmlessly off. The tank crew, lacking infantry support

Les Grands Bonfaits from the south. Ned Thornburn set up his HQ in the orchard; infantry were dug-in in the foreground.

The field where CSM Harrison 'shoved the PIAT through the hedge and pulled the blasted trigger'.

and in the deepening gloom of a summer's evening probably unaware of the source of the attack, promptly reversed some distance, then exited the Panther and stood outside the tank, looking around and talking in anxious whispers. Harrison renewed his hunt, but as he prepared a second shot, a bramble snared the front of the PIAT and the bomb dropped out of its cradle. 'That made me hopping mad,' Harrison recalled:

> '...so I stamped five yards down the road, yanked the brushwood out of the way, shoved the PIAT through the hedge and pulled the blasted trigger.'[6]

The bomb went off like a clap of thunder; the Panther was destroyed and its crew were not seen again. As luck would have it, Ned Thornburn was at that very moment discussing his situation over a radio link to his commanding officer (this time using the company 19 set, somewhat more reliable and with longer range than the 38). Thornburn was just pointing out that his Sherman support had pulled back and there were three Panthers close by, when the sound of the almighty explosion reached him.

> 'Ah! That was one of them going up! Yes, we'll stay here somehow.'
>
> 'Good man!' the CO responded. 'I'll send you some antitank guns and another couple of platoons.'

In this way, one man's enterprise turned a battle. In the short term, the destruction of one of their number led to the withdrawal of the other two enemy tanks and a quiet evening for D Company. More importantly, at a moment when Thornburn and his colonel might well have agreed to abandon the forward position, the destruction of 'Harrison's Panther' persuaded Ned Thornburn to remain on the hill. As he himself put it, 'Harrison's exploit gave me the will to chance my arm and play for the highest stakes.'

127

HOHENSTAUFEN: ROCK OF EMPERORS

The Hohenstaufen were a noble German family descended from dukes of Suabia and Franconia. They are best remembered for Frederick of Hohenstaufen who as Frederick I, 'Barbarossa' became Holy Roman Emperor in 1152. Frederick's thirty-eight-year reign was notable for his successful military campaigns in Poland, Hungary, and Bohemia, as well as his ongoing struggles with the papacy in Italy. A warrior to the last, the greatest of the Hohenstaufen dynasty died leading his army to join the Third Crusade, drowning in his heavy armour while crossing the river Calycadnus in Cilicia. 753 years later, another Hohenstaufen was fighting on the eastern boundaries of a German empire, this time an SS Panzer division in Galicia defending the eastern borders of Poland and Hungary against the armies of Russia.

Along with its sister *10 SS Panzerdivision 'Frundsberg'*, the *10 SS Panzerdivision 'Hohenstaufen'* returned to France at the end of June.

Following the fighting in the month of July around Caen, *Hohenstaufen's* strength was depleted to the point that reorganisation was called for. The division's two infantry regiments (*19. and 20. SS Panzergrenadier Regiments*) were recombined. Effectively, the men and equipment of two battalions, *I/20* and *II/20 SS Pz.Gr.Rgt.*, were absorbed into *19. SS Pz.Gr.Rgt.* which from 23 July became *9. SS Pz.Gr.Rgt. 'H'*. This left *20. SS Pz.Gr.Rgt.'s* third battalion. By 1944, with shortages biting, only one of the Panzer division's six infantry battalions was equipped with armoured personnel carriers (in the form of half-tracks). What survived of *III/20. SS Pz.Gr.Rgt.* with its half-track-borne infantry was placed under the direct command of Otto Meyer's *9. SS Panzer Regiment*. Apart from these half-tracks, as of 2 August, *Hohenstaufen's 9. SS Panzer Regiment* had a total of seventy-six armoured fighting vehicles: thirty one Panzer V 'Panther' tanks in its first battalion, seventeen Panzer IV, and twenty-eight *Sturmgeschütze* in its second. At the same time, support elements were brought up to strength with drafts from *SS Feldersatz-Bataillon 9*, and the division, originally recruited from Austria, counted itself lucky that most of these were 'Volksdeutsch', young ethnic Germans recruited from Hungarian and Yugoslavian areas.

TIGERS OF THE *HOHENSTAUFEN*

At 20.35 hours on 1 August, *9 SS Panzerdivision* received a situation report direct from an increasingly desperate *21 Panzerdivision*.

'Situation uncertain on our left wing and the neighbouring infantry division is insufficient. Enemy pushing in the direction la Ferronnière – Montchamp, with the spearhead north west of Montchamp. Also attacks on axis Bonneville – Jurques (spearpoint Jurques) and from Saint-Martin-des-Besaces on axis Saint-Denis – Maisoncelles – Letourneur (spearpoint la

Viville). When can you take place in the line?'

The order was clear: the division was to advance along the Vassy – Vire road and link up with *3 Fallschirmjägerdivision* on the extreme right of *Seventh Armee*, whose right flank was exposed by the widening gap between *Seventh Armee* and *Panzergruppe West. Hohenstaufen's* divisional plan was more detailed. To the extent that aerial reconnaissance was not going to be available, the plan had to be flexible; units would have to reconnoitre for themselves (and this was to shape the way events unfolded throughout a confused day). But in its simplest form, the plan was to encircle the apparent British breakthrough with two converging wings. One column would drive westwards, directly into the British flank, with the objective of securing le Bény-Bocage. The second wing would proceed clockwise around the breakthrough, passing through Vassy, proceeding west along the main highway to Vire, and then striking north up the main Vire – Caen road to close the encirclement at le Bény-Bocage and re form the front line, sealing off the threatened area.

The first wing, charged with driving straight into the British left flank, included the greater part of *Hohenstaufen*. In *Kampfgruppe* Meyer, SS-*Obersturmbannführer* Otto Meyer had under his command most of his own tank regiment (the second battalion with its mixture of Panzer IVs and assault guns, and the Panther-equipped first battalion); a small part of the divisional reconnaissance regiment; and the greater part of the divisional artillery. Also under his command was placed the remnants of *21 Panzerdivision*, operating to the north and covering *Hohenstaufen's* right flank.

The second wing was *Kampfgruppe Weiss*. This group was commanded

Panzergrenadiere mounted in SdKfz251/1 half-tracks.

The close bocage country was not ideal terrain for the Tiger.

by the recently-promoted *Sturmbannführer* Hans Weiss of *schwere SS Panzer Abteilung 102*. Not actually a member of *Hohenstaufen*, Weiss was nevertheless a friend of long standing. His heavy tank battalion, like most Tiger tank units in the West, was a corps-level asset which had lent support to *9. SS Panzerdivision* both in Russia and in Normandy. Through the month of July, *Battalion 102* had been fighting on the slopes of the infamous Hill

Tiger I of Weiss' *schwere SS-Panzer Abteilung* 102, proceeded by a captured Daimler scout car.

The aftermath of the British debacle at Villers-Bocage.

112 south of the Odon, engaging amongst others the tanks of 11th Armoured. The unit's Tiger I tanks were an earlier and lighter model than the 'King' Tigers of *s.Pz.Abt. 503*. But from the point of view of the British tank troops the difference was fairly academic. Both were mobile fortresses. The 75mm gun of British tanks was incapable of overcoming the frontal armour of either mark of Tiger, even at close range; while a hit by a Tiger's 8.8cm gun anywhere on any British armoured vehicle would almost certainly spell its utter destruction, regardless of range. Early in the Normandy campaign, a single Tiger I (of *s.SS-Pz.Abt. 101*) commanded by SS-*Obersturmführer* Michael Wittmann was credited with destroying over twenty-five armoured vehicles and single-handedly stopping 7th Armoured Division in its tracks. The truth was somewhat different. A variety of German units had contributed to the debacle at Villers-Bocage. The story was a masterpiece of German propaganda, further inflated by trick photography for the pages of 'Signal' magazine and by the promotion of Wittman to celebrity status. But even the truth was bad enough. The famous Desert Rats had suffered a humiliating defeat. The story spread, and increasingly thereafter the name 'Tiger' spread apprehension among Allied tank crews.

Nominally equipped with forty-five Tiger tanks, no replacements had been received by *102. Abteilung* since its arrival in Normandy, nor were any to be forthcoming. (Only on 20 August were six replacement tanks in Germany earmarked for the battalion, but by that time the unit had virtually ceased to exist and the tanks were instead allocated to *s.SS-Pz.Abt. 103*.) In fact, by 30 July there were only sixty Tiger Is operational in the

An early model, short-barrel 7.5cm *Sturmgeschütz III.*

Sturmgeschütz III with the long 7.5cm antitank gun.

whole of Normandy. On that date, *102. Abt.* had thirty Tigers operational, a further twelve in field workshops awaiting repair. (By 5 August, this was to fall to a total of only twenty, all more-or-less operational.) In addition to the Tigers, *Kampfgruppe* Weiss took command from 2 August of the greater part of *Hohenstaufen's* reconnaissance regiment, a powerful and highly mobile unit containing both armoured car and half-track companies.

STURMGESCHÜTZE AT MONTCHAUVET

One of the first units of *Hohenstaufen's Kampfgruppe* Meyer into action on this front was the seventh company of the division's tank regiment. *7./SS Pz-Rgt. 9* was one of the many 'tank' companies of the 1944 German army actually equipped with assault guns, in this case the *Sturmgeschütz III.*

The German *Sturmgeschütze* were originally created to provide close artillery support for army infantry regiments. The first models of *Sturmgeschütz III* were derived from obsolescent *Panzer III* battle tanks. Freed of the constraint of a rotating turret, a much larger gun could be mounted low in the hull. With the weight of the turret removed, heavier frontal armour could be carried. Also the overall height of the vehicle was reduced by almost a quarter. As target height is a critical factor in antitank range finding, the lower profile made the *Sturmgeschütz* not only easier to hide but also harder to hit once its position was revealed. In an infantry support role, crewed by élite artillery troops, it proved an efficient as well as highly cost-effective weapon, employed tactically as a mobile reserve capable of overwhelming enemy defences with massed, short-range artillery fire. As the war progressed, its effectiveness grew and its role widened. The early short-barrelled, 7.5cm direct-fire assault cannon were replaced not only by considerably more powerful 10.5cm howitzers, but more commonly by long, high-velocity 7.5cm guns which made the *Sturmgeschütz* effective in an antitank role.

As the war progressed and pressure on German industrial resources grew, shortcuts were adopted. By 1944, even the favoured SS divisions had to accept a proportion of their battle tanks being replaced with assault guns. And for all its strengths, when employed as a tank the *Sturmgeschütz* was decidedly second rate. The lack of a turret capable of fairly rapid traverse through a 360 degree arc was a major shortcoming in fluid tactical situations, in which enemy tanks or guns could emerge from any direction. In a tank, the commander would order the gunner sitting directly in front of him to traverse the turret onto a heading. In an assault gun, the commander had first to contact the driver down in his front-hull position and have him rotate the entire vehicle onto the approximate heading required, while the gunner in his turn struggled to acquire the target in the narrow field of his telescopic sights. Needless to say, this was a more lengthy procedure. Even if the Maybach engine was running, consuming precious fuel, the process would be time-consuming. (Turreted tanks could traverse their turrets manually, though it should be pointed out that most German tanks of the period could only use their power traverse with engines running.) If the engine had to be started up, there was yet more risk not only of the target being lost but also of giving away the assault gun's position and losing the advantage of surprise.

In the attack, protection of the weaker side and rear armour was harder to achieve. In defence, while a turreted tank could be 'dug-in' with only its rotating (and more thickly armoured) turret exposed, a dug-in assault gun could hardly turn at all without relinquishing its entrenchment altogether. The lower profile afforded by lack of a turret, hitherto so useful, proved in Normandy to be a major problem when the assault guns were faced with the high, dense hedgerows of the bocage country.[7] This was not so great a difficulty when operating defensively, so long as there was time for adequate reconnoitring of sites that would give the assault guns a good field of fire. Finally, while assault guns were designed for close infantry support, the corollary was that they depended even more than the tanks on having infantry nearby to protect them from enemy infantry and anti-tank guns. The *Sturmartillerie* manual made clear that, while not coming too close to the *Sturmgeschütz* (which was likely to be a magnet for enemy fire), nevertheless:

> 'Troops co-operating with Sturmgeschütze must give all possible support in dealing with mines and other obstacles... The moral support which the infantry receives through its presence is important...' but, it has no facilities for defending itself at close quarters.'[8]

The early German assault guns lacked any machine guns, relying on nearby infantry for small-arms support; later models of the *Sturmgeschütz III* had a machine gun, usually externally mounted so that the loader had to be exposed (and of course not fulfilling his primary role inside) in order to operate it.

Whenever the relative merits of German tanks of the Second World War are considered, it should be remembered that the excellence of such tanks as the Panther and Tiger came at a heavy price. Individually unsurpassed, these tanks drew heavily on resources that the Third Reich could ill afford. For all their qualitative superiority, their numbers could never keep pace with the Sherman and T34 tanks streaming off American and Soviet production lines, and the *Heer* had increasingly to dilute its armoured regiments with assault guns. Inexorably, tactical employment of the *Sturmgeschütz* broadened: from a specialist infantry support weapon to a general antitank role, and ultimately as a substitute for battle tanks.

Notwithstanding its limitations, the *Sturmgeschütz III* nevertheless proved its worth in the hands of the *9. SS Panzer Regiment*, and by the end of July had accumulated substantial combat experience on the banks of the

German infantry in the early morning mist.

Odon River and the slopes of Hills 112 and 113. It was a handful of these *Sturmgeschütze* standing guard in a farmyard south of Montchauvet in the small hours of 2 August which formed the vanguard of the newly-arriving division. In the pre-dawn glow there arrived a handful of German infantry. These were stragglers from the *752. Grenadier Regiment*, part of the shattered *326. Infanteriedivision*. Numbering only thirteen men, some of whom had abandoned their weapons, this little band had been taken under the wing of a captain of *Feldgendarmerie* – the military police known as *Kettenhunde* ('chain-dogs') by virtue of their distinctive gorget-plate insignia worn on a metal chain around the neck. Not just traffic policemen, though they fulfilled this role most effectively throughout the Normandy campaign, these field police were characterized by their ruthlessness. Almost to the war's end, disaffection and desertion in the ranks were kept under control by the certainty of harsh punishment. On the Eastern front it was not unknown for German troops on the line of march to see fellow soldiers hanging at the roadside where they had been summarily executed for some breach of military discipline.

The captain of *Feldgendarmerie* agreed to wait with the three *Sturmgeschütze* to see what would develop. Before long, the remainder of *Obersturmführer* Fröhlich's 7. *Kompanie* of *Sturmgeschütze* arrived on the scene, likewise accompanied by infantry stragglers. And then the transformation began. Once again, the resilience of the German army in Normandy was illustrated as a band of infantrymen, some unarmed, all lacking tactical direction, their parent units smashed, were quickly re-formed into an effective unit. Where the vital squad machine guns were lacking these were provided by the *Sturmgeschütz* crews, who readily sacrificed their vehicles' external MG34s in exchange for effective infantry support. (Unlike the British Army, German vehicles' machine guns were generally interchangeable with those of the infantry.) From a handful of routed infantry and assault guns was forged the spearhead of an SS Panzer division's advance. *Kampfgruppe* Fröhlich was operational, ready to march south west towards Montchamp in search of an enemy.

WELSH GUARDS ACROSS THE SOULEUVRE

By 1943, it was clear that the American Sherman tank was going to be the mainstay of the British armoured divisions in the invasion of northwest Europe. However, the War Office was still struggling to find an acceptable, domestically manufactured 'cruiser' tank, and by 1944 the new Cromwell was in production. Descended from a line of cruiser tanks whose battleworthiness varied from just acceptable to downright appalling, the Cromwell was not universally welcomed by the armoured divisions. In fact, it was to prove one of the more successful British designs of the war. While the Cromwell was no match for 1944-vintage German battle tanks, neither was the Sherman. Compared to the Sherman, the Cromwell was acceptable in most respects and even superior in some. It had a good turn of speed, was reliable, its main gun proved especially responsive in laying and firing, and it was somewhat less prone to burning.

Each of VIII Corps' armoured divisions was assigned a regiment of Cromwells, and to these was given the role of close tactical reconnaissance on the divisional front. This unit replaced the previous armoured car regiment, which now became a Corps-level asset. Some queried the need for change; 'Pip' Roberts 'never understood the reason' and by the time of BLUECOAT he had reverted to using the Cromwells as battle tanks and the armoured cars of the Household Cavalry for reconnaissance. The armoured cars continued to justify his confidence, providing a valued service in front of 11th Armoured Division. As for the Cromwells, their early experiences in Normandy were not happy ones. 11th Armoured Division's Cromwell regiment, 2/Northamptonshire Yeomanry, performed valiantly throughout Operations EPSOM and GOODWOOD, but the terrain simply was not suitable for lightly armoured tanks to operate independently of infantry. In the case of the Northants Yeomanry, there was the further indignity of their unfamiliar tanks occasionally being fired on by friendly Shermans, and they had more hardships to endure during BLUECOAT.

Cromwell tanks of the Welsh Guards in Normandy.

Guards Armoured Division was still intending to employ its Cromwell regiment, 2/Armoured Reconnaissance Regiment Welsh Guards, in the designated reconnaissance role. Never was this more needed than on the morning of 2 August. Guards Armoured's orders for the day ('ambitious', most of the division felt) were to make for Vassy, almost twenty kilometres from the Souleuvre bridge as the crow flies, and in actuality much further along winding country roads. The division was to follow as the Welsh Guards' Cromwell tanks reconnoitred the road ahead. However, the early hours of 2 August found the Welsh Guards far from the front line. At 02.00 hours, 2 Company and 'X' Company of 3/Irish Guards ventured past le Tourneur. They found the place empty of Germans and the bridge (still!) intact. As so often in Normandy, instead of destroying a bridge to slow the Allies' advance, the retreating Germans had preferred to leave the bridge outside le Tourneur unblown to facilitate a future counter attack. The way appeared open, and the divisional reconnaissance units were called for. But they were not to hand. The armoured cars of the attached Inns of Court Regiment and the division's own Welsh Guards had spent the night far behind the lines, still north of St-Martin-des-Besaces. It was the best the Welsh Guards' Cromwells could do to cross the bridge at le Tourneur at dawn, reaching Cathéolles soon after. By then, 11th Armoured Division infantry had departed and instead of a friendly welcome, the point unit of Guards Armoured Division came under enemy fire. Later, when the Inns of Court arrived, three of their lightly-armoured cars were quickly lost to mortar fire and mines in the steep-sided ravine south of Cathéolles.

True to its reconnaissance role, the Welsh Guards split into three probing columns. 1 Squadron set out due east along the narrow valley of the Rubec stream towards Montchauvet. 2 Squadron explored the division's left flank, north east along the main road towards Villers-Bocage. And on the right flank, 3 Squadron headed south on that same road, hoping to make good progress in the wake of 11th Armoured as far as la Ferronnière and thereafter to strike eastwards across country towards St-Charles-de-Percy and Montchamp.

N◄—

The narrow valley of the Rubec, 500m east of 'mortar gulch'.

The Cromwells of 1 Squadron crossed the Cathéolles bridge and, entering 'mortar gulch', and turning sharply, plunged up the narrow valley of the Rubec stream. This was not tank country. There was no room to deploy: with the stream to their right and a steep wooded slope on their left, they could only advance in a single column along the country lane that followed the meanders of the river valley. Lines of sight were short; every turn in the road was a potential ambush. Without infantry to probe the road ahead and the wooded slopes above, the Cromwells were entirely

Hidden German gun

Approaching this bend, the lead 1 Squadron Cromwell was hit by by a gun emplaced below the far horizon.

vulnerable to any prepared defence. And the survivors of *326. Infanteriedivision* had now returned to the fray. The column was barely two miles out of Cathéolles when a hidden German gun demolished the lead tank, just short of the junction with a lane leading north up a side valley to la Cour and Hill 220 [modern 216]. Burning with its crew, the Cromwell completely blocked the narrow lane. Some followers tried to force a passage but none succeeded. With difficulty, the column reversed direction and returned to Cathéolles. 2 Squadron fared little better. Barely two miles up the dead straight highway, they too were stopped short by well entrenched German infantry and guns, whereupon they too reported their mission to be impossible. Both 1 and 2 Squadrons accepted orders to move south in support of 3 Squadron.

3 Squadron Welsh Guards made a good start, shrugging off the artillery fire directed on 'mortar gulch' and proceeding along the highway to la Ferronnière, where they turned left on the road for Montchamp. It was now about 06.00 hours; the morning was well advanced, and the *Sturmgeschütze* and infantry of *Kampfgruppe* Fröhlich had made good time advancing west from Montchauvet. Finding Montchamp clear of enemies, they had sent part of their force ahead to St-Charles-de-Percy. Here, they deployed across the path of the Welsh Guards. Once again, the first the unaccompanied tanks knew of the German presence was antitank shells tearing into the Cromwells. Fröhlich's detachment claimed to have destroyed a total of five tanks and captured five half-tracks (which were later put to use as

139

ammunition carriers). With no realistic chance of taking the small town, 3 Squadron took advantage of a track which by-passed the north side of St Charles towards a small bridge, from which the Cromwells struck east along the Souleuvre valley. Once clear of the German-held town, 3 Squadron drove across country towards Montchamp. Here, the story was repeated. Approaching a small bridge by a road junction just short of Montchamp, the column came under fire from more of Fröhlich's *Sturmgeschütze* and a further Cromwell was lost. (Fröhlich himself was now in Montchamp, having been injured in the first exchange of fire at St

3 Squadron Welsh Guards vs KG Frölich

St-Charles-de-Percy

Chateau

River Souleuvre

Montchamp

0   250m

N

The passage through 'mortar gulch' on the way to Vire.

Charles and taken back to Montchamp to be treated in an aid station set up in the schoolhouse there.) The column of Cromwells turned away from the town, this time southwards, and again picked its way across reasonably open country, eventually stopping and harbouring for the rest of the day around the hamlet of la Marvindière. Later in the morning, 1 and 2 Squadrons came up, and were deployed around the nearby hamlets of Friouse and Cavignaux.

The Guards' reconnaissance regiment had done its job. The Cromwells had pressed forward, located the enemy, and the regiment established itself ahead of the Guards Armoured Division's intended axis of advance. But its position was isolated and vulnerable, with known enemy units covering the roads to the rear and threatening resupply. By sheer good fortune, friendly infantry ended the day nearby. On the extreme left flank of 11th Armoured Division, a company of British infantry of 4/KSLI had established an outpost around the hilltop farm of les Grands Bonfaits, and by day's end were securely dug-in.

GUARDS ARMOURED AND KG MEYER

As to the rest of Guards Armoured, once again, the main striking force of the division was organised into the Grenadier and Irish groups. The Grenadier group of 2/(Armoured) Grenadier and 1/(Motor) Grenadier Guards began their day with an 08.00 hours attack east out of Cathéolles. Their Sherman tanks entered the narrow Rubec valley with infantry out on either flank, just as the Cromwells of 1 Squadron, Welsh Guards were pulling out. The Grenadiers' commander briefly reconsidered his mission in light of the Welsh Guards' unhappy experience, but decided to continue. The terrain was unpromising, but the prospect of reaching Montchauvet and securing a pivot for the rest of the division to advance around was too great. Unfortunately for the Guards, every hour that passed made that goal less achievable.

Through the night, the Rubec valley had been almost undefended. By dawn, elements of *326. Division* arrived to set up defences, and were just in time to put a stop to the Cromwells' early foray. Just as the Welsh Guards were falling back up the valley, elements of *9. SS Panzerdivision* arrived, including more armour of the *2/9. SS-Pz.Rgt.* Less than half way to Montchauvet, the Guards' advance was stopped dead by three Panzer IV tanks of 6 *Kompanie, SS Pz.Rgt. 9*, under SS-*Obersturmführer* Grimm. With the defenders further stiffened by elements of *Hohenstaufen's* Regiment 'H', local counter attacks ensured that the high ground east of Cathéolles remained in German hands. The fighting was desperate as newly-arriving SS Panzer Grenadiers reinvigorated tiring infantrymen of *326. Division*. At one point a single despatch runner, SS-*Sturmann* Hermann Alber, took command of nine *326. Division* soldiers and in the confusion not only re-took Hill 221, but pressed on down its slopes to la Vautelière where in a frenzied attack he personally destroyed a Cromwell tank with grenades.

Tanks and infantry of both sides contested the hills dominating both banks of the Rubec stream. To the north, the Germans held Arclais and with it Hill 221, even coming down off the hill to throw the Guards back from the Villers-Bocage road. To the south of the Rubec, the Germans on Hill 176 resisted all efforts to take the hamlets of Drouet and l'Auteloy. In so doing, they denied the direct road up the valley to Montchauvet. Moreover they preserved the northern flank of Hill 270, north of St-Charles-de-Percy and Montchamp (where *Kampfgruppe* Fröhlich was established, covering the hill's southern flank). From the dominating heights of Hill 270, guns and mortars kept the main road between Cathéolles and la Ferronnière under constant fire and exacted a particularly heavy toll of Guards officers as their vehicles ran the gauntlet of 'mortar gulch'.

While the Grenadier Group contested the heights above the Rubec valley, the Irish Group of 2/(Armoured) Irish and 5/Coldstream Guards was stuck in the area of Cathéolles. Only later in the day was the road cleared sufficiently for its move south. Even so, the passage of 'mortar gulch' cost the 5/Coldstream their second commanding officer in two days. Like the 2/Welsh Guards, the leading elements of the Irish Group first tried to break through St-Charles-de-Percy and were stopped by a German force advancing westwards. Unlike the Welsh Guards, it was not just *Kampfgruppe* Fröhlich that they had run into, but an advance unit of *Hohenstaufen Panzergrenadiere*, under no less pressure to gain ground to the west than were the Guards to move south. Having blunted the German advance (and so saved the rear echelon of 11th Armoured Division from potential disaster), the Irish group moved on, taking a southerly heading across country. Fortuitously, they avoided any further pockets of resistance, harbouring at day's end close to la Marvindière. Though within a few fields of the 2/Welsh Guards, in the dense farmland neither formation realised the other was nearby until morning.

Later in the day, responding to urgent appeals from VIII Corps, Guards Armoured launched 3/Irish Guards across the Souleuvre, through 'mortar gulch', and on to reach the relative calm of la Ferronnière just as night was falling. The column attempted to push on further in the darkness to reach St-Charles-de-Percy, but was stopped by reinforced elements of *Kampfgruppe* Fröhlich just east of la Ferronnière, where their commander decided to halt for the night.

On its formation in the small hours of the morning, *Kampfgruppe* Fröhlich had set out towards the divisional objective of le

SS-*Obersturmbannführer* Otto Meyer

Bény-Bocage. Through the day, it had withstood successive waves of British armour sweeping its strongpoints. By evening, the remains of *7./SS Pz.Rgt. 9* and the survivors of its infantry escort clung to the villages of St-Charles-de-Percy and Montchamp. The small unit now formed an outpost blocking any British night moves, and also fulfilled the useful role of guarding the flank of the German gun positions on Hill 270, which in turn continued to interdict the main Villers-Bocage to Vire road. Come morning, *Kampfgruppe* Fröhlich would fall back from its forward positions and be subsumed within the larger *Kampfgruppe* Meyer.

Representing the major part of *9. SS Panzerdivision*, *Kampfgruppe* Meyer had fallen well short of its objective of retaking le Bény-Bocage. By evening, its *I. Bataillon SS-Pz.Gr.Rgt.* 'H' had progressed only as far west as Maisoncelle, just south of Montchamp. Further south, *1/9. SS-Pz.Rgt.* with its Panther tanks had taken its toll of British tanks, but had failed to make the territorial gains its orders required. Only in small parties of company strength or less had the *Panzergrenadiere* of Regiment 'H' and the

143

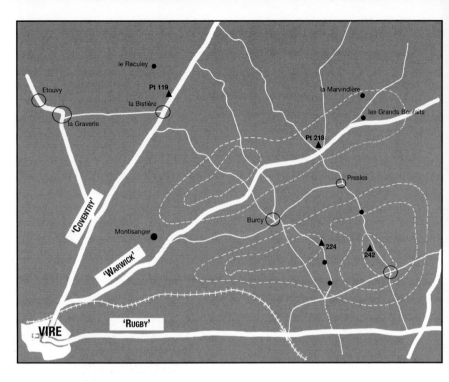

reconnaissance vehicles of Gräbner's *Aufklärungs Abteilung* managed to infiltrate west into the battle zone. Nevertheless, these small probing bands had sounded a warning of what was to befall 11th Armoured Division in the days to come. Already, British soft-skinned supply vehicles advancing through the night to rendezvous with their fighting units were being ambushed. Some time later, a German supply column driven into a village held by Guards Armoured Division was found to contain a water truck captured from 2/Welsh Guards and a petrol lorry from 2/Irish Guards. Further south, despatch riders from the Monmouths' defensive 'box' set off north across the Burcy valley and were not seen again. With opposing armoured spearheads literally crossing each others' paths, resupplying the forward British units threatened to become problematic.

On 2 August, both Guards Armoured Division and *Kampfgruppe* Meyer had ambitious objectives which proved impossible to achieve. The Guards regiments were struggling to come to terms with new tactics, fighting in a new and unaccustomed terrain against a ferociously determined enemy, whilst trying to funnel an entire armoured division down a single road under heavy fire. By the end of the day, it was no small achievement to have projected a single group of three battalions (2/Welsh reconnaissance, 3/Irish tanks, and 5/Coldstream infantry) somewhere close to the otherwise open left flank of 11th Armoured Division. Even though cut off from their parent division (the tactical headquarters of both Guards

Armoured Division's two brigades ended the day still north of le Tourneur), these units were in the right place to protect the British breakthrough. For this, 11th Armoured might have been grateful, had they only known that Guardsmen were there! For their part, the Germans were constrained not so much by inexperience as by their piecemeal arrival in an unfamiliar and unreconnoitred sector of the front. Low-level leaders had to assess an uncertain situation and react to whatever they discovered. Lacking clear knowledge of the British positions or strength, *Kampfgruppe* Meyer was restricted to feeling its way forward on a broad front. But its force grew as the day passed. A German line took shape as the main force of SS-*Obersturmführer* Zollhöfer's *SS-Pz.Gr.Rgt.* 'H' shook itself out from marching column into a battle line from the bastion of Hill 270 southwards through Montchamp to Estry. Steadily, the German pressure increased along the vulnerable flank of the British breakthrough.

11TH ARMOURED DIGS IN AS *KG* WEISS REACHES VIRE

By nightfall, the fighting units of 11th Armoured Division were established in good defensive positions. Yet the position of 11th Armoured was far from secure. During the afternoon it had become clear to 'Pip' Roberts, in his tactical headquarters at le Reculey, that the advance had progressed far enough. The 'horns' of the Black Bull division were its tank regiments. These were had plunged deep into enemy territory, and had paid a price. Of the division's 145 Sherman tanks ready for action at the end of 1 August, thirty-one were reported lost at the end of the day; six of these the vital, 17-pounder armed Fireflies. And the Black Bull's left flank was a concern. Fresh in Roberts' mind was the recent memory of GOODWOOD, where the delayed arrival of Guards Armoured Division had led to his division's left flank becoming dangerously exposed. Then, he had pushed on and taken heavy losses. Now, Roberts worried about the fluid situation of his rear areas. He frankly dreaded the thought of German armour rampaging among the transport columns that were the life blood of his fighting units.

Yet another legacy of GOODWOOD influenced 'Pip' Roberts. Barely a week previously, on 24 July, an 11th Armoured Division conference had been held to review lessons learned from the GOODWOOD battle. One of the first of these was that the final objective should have been a topographical feature. That was to say, an advance should come to a halt on ground that lent itself to being held:

> '...finishing on a tactical feature on which either hull down or covered positions could be occupied'.

As things stood at the end of 2 August, the two principal battle groups of the division were established on substantial ridge lines, offering both visibility over the enemy and the relative shelter of the reverse slope. And

'We were pushing the engines hard.'

as the final consideration, in its present positions the entire force of 11th Armoured Division was still within the protective umbrella of VIII Corps' artillery. Roberts determined that there would be no further advance.

Late in the afternoon, O'Connor visited Roberts at le Reculey and, as luck would have it, the general's arrival was heralded by a German artillery strike. Nothing could have been more convincing in support of Roberts' argument. 11th Armoured Division would hold its ground. What is more, O'Connor promised infantry reinforcements in the shape of 185 Brigade from 3rd (Infantry) Division. By 22.30 hours, the division's armoured regiments were receiving the order to hold the ground they were on.

While 11th Armoured Division was putting on the brakes, *Kampfgruppe* Weiss was pushing forward hard. SS-*Sturmbannführer* Hans Weiss's own unit of Tiger tanks had experienced a nightmare journey even to reach the battle area. Setting off after nightfall from their ambush positions on the southern slopes of Hill 112, they drove their 60-ton monsters through the hours of darkness along winding country roads already jammed with west-bound traffic. With the dawn came the added burden of constant watchfulness for signs of an imminent air raid. Their plan was to route southwards from Estry to join the main highway for a straight run west into Vire.

Passing through Estry, it seems that *Obersturmführer* Kalls's leading *1. Kompanie* decided in mid-afternoon to try a short cut, taking a right turn off the main southbound road to head towards Chênedollé. Shortly after, Kalls reported that he had run into a British armoured spearhead, and had

146

destroyed a number of British tanks. His claim was no exaggeration: it was these Tiger tanks that had crushed the 23/Hussars' A Squadron.[9] But Weiss's travel arrangements had not allowed for an encounter with enemy armour so far south. Like other German commanders that day, he and his subordinates had to update their plans in light of developments. We can safely assume that the tank engaged by the 8/RB PIATs in Chênedollé was likewise a Tiger of *s.SS Pz.Abt. 102* as the column probed to find a clear route to Vire. Weiss was not looking for a fight so far from his objective. But he could not ignore the threat when his was the only available force in the area. Recognising that a major British armoured breakthrough must have taken place, and with no other force immediately to hand, Weiss ordered his *1. Kompanie*, under Kalls, to take up defensive positions around Chênedollé. This left his *2. Kompanie* led by *Untersturmführer* Schroif to complete the battalion's primary mission.

A third time Weiss's *Kampfgruppe* probed west, this time along the main highway to Vire. A third time British tanks lay across their path, this time Steel Brownlie's Fife and Forfars. Turning west from the crossroads at les Hauts Vents and advancing well spaced along the highway, the Tiger tanks' 8.8cm guns firing from over two thousand metres easily outranged the Fife and Forfars' Shermans. For all Steel Brownlie's jubilation at the dramatic arrival of the Typhoon fighter-bombers, Schroif's company survived their attack. One of the Tiger tank commanders of *2. Kompanie*, *Unterscharführer* Ernst Streng recalled:

> 'Bullets rattled against the turret of my tank and great sheets of fire and smoke billowed up where the rockets had hit the ground. Time and again they screamed down on us. Then the attack stopped as abruptly as it had started.'

The 'tiffies' did little physical damage to the Tiger tanks. Though the sixty-pound rockets packed an awesome punch, they were extremely inaccurate and direct hits on tanks were rare. But the air attack was not in vain. As a direct consequence, Streng relates, 'Schroif decided to make a detour. We turned back and moved further south'. *KG* Weiss had been persuaded that the direct highway to Vire was not an option. Instead, Schroif's company turned back to the Hauts Vents crossroads and detoured south on the Tinchebray road before turning north again for Vire. Time was lost. The company of heavy tanks did not arrive in Vire until 20.35 hours (21.35

147

Allied time), and reached the northern suburbs only just in time to see last of the Northants Yeomanry's Cromwells driving off. The extra distance had cost more than time. A night and a day of grinding forward had worn out the heavy vehicles as well as their crews. Streng again:

> 'The Panzers of Reisske and Münster broke down and had to be left at the roadside. We were pushing the engines hard. That and the warm summer evening was causing them to overheat.'

The second major element of *Kampfgruppe* Weiss was *Hohenstaufen's* reconnaissance battalion. This unit resembled neither the Cromwell-equipped Welsh Guards nor the Household Cavalry with its light armoured cars. *9. SS Panzer Aufklärungs Abteilung* was a mixed force of well armed and fast armoured vehicles and infantry. Its five companies included two PSW companies ('*Panzerspähwagen*', or 'armoured probing vehicles'), the first equipped with light, fast armoured cars and the second with turreted half-tracks. Two SPW companies ('*Schützenpanzerwagen*') were composed of soldiers mounted in small, armoured half-track personnel carriers. A fifth heavy weapons company mounted in medium half-tracks included support guns, antitank guns, and engineers. While specialising in reconnaissance, for which speed was more important than firepower, this battalion could also muster the resilience to hold the line and even the brute force to conduct armoured assaults. Led by the charismatic *Hauptsturmführer* Viktor-Eberhard Gräbner, the unit had successfully made the transition from the open Russian steppe to the Normandy bocage. In mid-July, Gräbner's battalion had been flung into the line to stabilise the front at Noyers, where the German *277 Division* was hard pressed by the British 59th (Infantry) Division. In a series of energetic counter attacks, the *9. SS Panzer Aufklärungs Abteilung* succeeded in pushing the British out of Noyers. For the particularly daring dawn attack on 15 July, Gräbner himself was recommended for the *Ritterkreuz*, the Knight's Cross (which decoration he was actually to receive on 17 September, the day before he disappeared leading a failed charge over the Arnhem bridge against British paratroops).

Gräbner's unit was the most mobile element of *Kampfgruppe* Weiss. About 16:00 hours on 2 August, Gräbner's headquarters was at Estry. But long before, advance parties from the battalion had been infiltrating the roads from Estry towards Vire. It was not Gräbner's style to take the same roundabout route as the heavy Tiger tanks, and through the day elements of *9. SS Panzer Aufklärungs Abteilung* ranged the country lanes across the path of the advancing British. As we have seen, vehicles of the *2. PSW Kompanie* had already fallen to the guns of the advancing 23/Hussars and 2/Fife and Forfar Yeomanry. As the day wore on, men and half-tracks of the *3. SPW Kompanie* penetrated the British rear areas around Presles and Burcy, as evidenced by the fate of Steel Brownlie's A Squadron. Using

148

speed and cover, small groups of reconnaissance vehicles penetrated as far as the outskirts of Vire, and by 19.00 hours were able to confirm that the town of Vire, though devastated, was still free of the enemy. Entering the town, they made contact with antiaircraft troops of *3 Fallschirmjägerdivision*. The gap blown between two German armies when Dickie's bridge fell to the British had begun to close.

THE END OF THE DAY

This was a day in which two major armoured forces effectively moved across each other's line of advance: the British from north to south; the Germans from east to west. The picture was utterly confused. If at the end of the day the fog of war could have rolled aside, both sides would probably have been horrified to find pockets of friendly and enemy troops interspersed across the rolling countryside. Anyone drawing a 'front line' across the battlefield map was deluding themselves. In such circumstances, the British were arguably at a disadvantage. Up to now, the British had fought the Normandy campaign as a series of set-piece battles, interspersed with day-to-day skirmishing around fairly constant front lines. Certainly the fluid situation that developed on 2 August was not to Montgomery's liking. Out of his depth and uncomfortable in fluid, fast-changing action, he preferred to

***General der Fallschirmjäger* Meindl with his Army commander Hausser.**

fight a 'tidy' battle in which he could maintain strict control. Conversely, many an officer and NCO in the German army had experience of being 'cut off' by enemy envelopment. Time after time in the open battlefields of Russia, Germans had proved their ability to survive encirclement and to break out from pockets.

While *II SS Panzer Korps* strove to reduce the threatening British salient south of Caumont, the pressure from further west had not slackened. Tanks of US 9th Armored Division were now reported in the area of St-Martin-

Don (8km west of le Bény-Bocage). *Heeresgruppe B* had little alternative but to authorise the further retreat of Meindl's *II Fallschirmjäger Korps* to a line extending from Beaumesnil (just north west of Vire) to Carville (between le Bény-Bocage and Roberts' 11th Armoured head-quarters at le Reculey). Meindl had already received stern warnings from his superiors to think only about his front and not to 'look over his shoulder'. But Meindl was soldier enough to know that failing to garrison Vire had been a strategic error. He later recorded his concerns that his whole corps was nearly isolated: 'What a day of crisis! What an opportunity for some English tank formation commander!'[10] By day's end, the immediate crisis was over. By midnight, the two antiaircraft batteries which had stood alone against the Northants Yeomanry Cromwells were reinforced by Meindl's paratroops and Weiss's Tiger tanks.

The news from Gräbner's reconnaissance half-tracks that Vire was still in German hands was welcome indeed to SS-*Obergruppenführer* Bittrich of *II SS Panzer Korps*. His superiors at *Panzergruppe West* headquarters had been thrown into confusion by an early-evening BBC news bulletin claiming that British formations had reached Vire. At last, Bittrich was able to reassure General Eberbach that this disaster had been forestalled. As the night progressed, Weiss's Tiger tanks arrived from the south and elements of Meindl's paratroop corps falling back from the north west joined to secure the town. Vire was no longer ripe for the plucking. The jaws of a German trap were set to close on le Bény-Bocage.

Reference

1 Bishop, p 71.
2 Bell, p 34.
3 McKee, p 334; 23rd Hussars, p 93.
4 23/Hussars, p 94.
5 *And Came Safely Home*, W Steel Brownlie, p 26.
6 Thornburn, p 109.
7 *Panzertruppen* volume 2: 1943-1945, Thomas L Jentz, 1996, ISBN 0-7643-0080-6, p 184.
8 'Instructions for the Employment of Sturmartillerie, 1940 & 1942' quoted in *Sturmgeschütz Assault Gun 1940-42*, Hilary Doyle and Tom Jentz, 1996, ISBN 1-85532-537-3.
9 *The History of the 12.SS-Panzerdivision Hitlerjugend*, Hubert Meyer, 1994, ISBN 0-921991-18-5, p 164.
10 How, p 92.

CHAPTER SEVEN

Thursday 3 August –
NO MAN'S LAND TO THE REAR

THE HIGH COMMAND

The two brigade groups of 11th Armoured Division had received the stop order. 29th Brigade passed on the message: 'Regts ordered to hold the ground they are on'. 23/Hussars and 8/RB were holding le Bas Perrier, supported by 119 Battery of 75/Antitank Regiment and six AVREs, while 3/RTR and 4/KSLI held Point 218 and les Grands Bonfaits. 159 Brigade likewise remained halted north of the line of the Vire-Vassy road, recording in the brigade War Diary that:

> '...owing to the US Army on our right and the Gds Arm Div on the left being slow in conforming to our line... positions were chosen for all round defence... The country is extremely close and moving off roads very difficult... It became apparent that until the left flank was cleared up a further advance would NOT be possible.'

Content with the progress of 11th Armoured and trusting in Guards Armoured and 15th Scottish to secure their breakthrough, Montgomery's attention passed to the slow progress of XXX Corps. The failure of that Corps to reach the dominating peak of Mont Pinçon raised awkward questions. Was the whole BLUECOAT advance threatened? And most particularly, had 7th Armoured Division, the famous 'Desert Rats', again failed? This was the day when the patience of Montgomery and Dempsey ran out. XXX Corps GOC Lieutenant General Bucknall was sacked, followed shortly by the 7th Armoured commander Major General 'Bobby' Erskine and his Brigadier 'Loony' Hinde.

In his headquarters at la Roche-Guyon, *Oberbefehlshaber West*, Günther von Kluge was experiencing agonies of frustration. Shortly after midnight there arrived Adolf Hitler's personally

Bucknall and Dempsey. Bucknall appears cheerful in this June photograph, but, even then, Dempsey had his doubts concerning XXX Corps' commander.

signed order for a war-winning new offensive. Kluge was to move all Panzer divisions from the British sector to mount a massive attack westwards across the base of the Cotentin peninsula. From the detached perspective of the *Führerhauptquartier*, this move made excellent sense. In line with German tactical thinking, infantry would hold the line while the mobile strike force of the Panzers would be concentrated into a single, unstoppable *Schwerpunkt*. From Mortain, the Atlantic beaches were a mere thirty kilometres away. Once a hole was punched through the American lines and Avranches taken, the head of the American 'COBRA' would be amputated from its sources of supply; deprived of essential logistics the armoured spearheads would wither on the vine.

There were two problems with Hitler's plan. The first was the number of infantry divisions marked on the *Führer's* situation maps which were in reality mere shadows of their paper strengths. The mobile Panzer divisions had long since been drawn into shoring-up vital stretches of the defensive line. And even these élite formations were constrained by Allied air supremacy, making strategic movements only during the short Normandy summer nights. The second problem was that no one, least of all Kluge, dared confront the *Führer* with these truths.

The previous evening's scare of Vire falling had focused Kluge's mind on the town. Not only was Vire an essential waypoint for the new units arriving from southern France; the Vire-Vassy road now assumed a new importance as an essential artery for the *Führer's* counter attack plan. Increasingly concerned with the status of that vital route, Kluge called reinforcements to its defence. Noting that British armour been moved away from Caen, he ordered further forces to be stripped from that sector. One result was the creation of a mobile strike force composed of elements of *12 SS Panzerdivision 'Hitler Jugend'*. Designated *'Aufklärungsgruppe Olboeter'*, this force under SS-*Sturmbannführer* Erich Olboeter consisted of 2.*SS-Pz.Kompanie* (thirteen combat-ready Panther tanks under SS-*Obersturmführer.* Gaede); the infantry of *9. Kompanie SS Pz.Gr.Rgt. 26; 1. Batterie Artillerieregiment 12* (six *Wespe* self-propelled 10.5cm guns); and six eight-wheeled armoured cars. From 22.25 hours on 2 August, *AG Olboeter* was formally detached to *II SS Panzer Korps* and ordered to proceed to area east of Vire.

Meanwhile, *9. SS Panzerdivision* was to continue its own offensive.

The *Wespe* self-propelled 10.5cm gun took a number of forms; this model is the SdKfz 124, based on a Panzer II chassis.

Eberbach signalled to Bittrich that he was no longer so concerned with reaching le Bény-Bocage as with closing the gap in the German line and securing Vire. A new point was selected for the junction of *Seventh Army* and *Panzergruppe* West: la Bistière on the Vire-Bény-Bocage road. Accordingly, the whole axis of *KG* Meyer's advance was tilted southwards, towards 11th Armoured Division's bastions north of the Vire-Vassy road. This was to have serious consequences for the day's action.

THE VIRE-VASSY ROAD

At first light on 3 August, Steel Brownlie's troop was relieved of its lonely vigil on the Vire-Vassy road. The four tank crews gratefully returned to their regimental headquarters area hoping to enjoy a meal and a sleep. Breakfast was cooked and eaten, but hopes of sleep were rudely dashed. A Squadron was called forward in support of Jimmy Samson's lone troop guarding the road. Steel Brownlie had not heard the orders and led his troop back to the spot so recently vacated. 'This', he confessed, 'was a mistake'. There, the relieving troop of Fife and Forfars had been overrun, the troop leader's tank knocked out and the infantry nowhere to be seen. Steel Brownlie found his own troop stranded, and for a few minutes chaos reigned:

> '*All kinds of things were flying about... There were enemy infantry everywhere, ours had been overrun, Jimmy had been knocked out, Bill Hotblack got a grenade in his turret, and more casualties were coming every minute. We fired a lot of smoke, and ran for positions half a mile back, astride the road leading north to Burcy.*'[1]

In his account of the action, Steel Brownlie credits Major J J How with identifying the German attackers as *AG Olboeter*. In fact, *Olboeter's Aufklärungsgruppe* arrived on the Vire-Vassy road, together with *Heerespionier Bataillon 600*, only on the evening of 3 August. Steel Brownlie's opponents on that morning were *Hohenstaufen's* own tactical reserve force, *SS-Panzerpionierbatallion 9*, charged with establishing contact with Weiss and Gräbner on the left and pushing the British back from the road.[2] Unlike British pioneers, these were not so much specialist engineers as assault infantry, heavily armed and fully prepared to hold their place in the front line. (It is also possible that the first company of *Obersturmführer* Kalls's *1. Kompanie* passed this way in the early morning of 3 August, to rejoin its parent *Tiger Abteilung* in Vire.)

The rest of the day passed relatively quietly for Steel Brownlie. Summoned back to the all-round defensive position at Burcy, he accepted a farmer's offer of a glass of calvados. The apple brandy mixed with the Benzedrine he had taken earlier and, in an extremity of fatigue, he began to hallucinate:

> '*I decided to go forward to the next hedge for a better view: "Driver*

He accepted a farmer's offer of a drink of calvados.

advance." *I woke to find that we had gone across several fields, and if there had been an alert Tiger in Presles he would have brewed up a Sherman with a sleeping commander.'*

KAMPFGRUPPE WEISS

SS-Sturmbannführer. Weiss now had his Tiger Battalion assembled in Vire, together with the greater part of *Hauptsturmführer.* Gräbner's reconnaissance battalion. The first priority was to reach la Bistière, the designated rendezvous with *Kampfgruppe* Meyer. Shortly after midday (13.00 hours, British time) a mixed column set off on its five kilometre advance. Nine Tiger tanks led the way, astride the main road, followed by a *Zug* (platoon) of Gräbner's infantry, their small reconnaissance half-tracks dwarfed by the heavy tanks, and a pair of self-propelled antiaircraft guns.

The 2/Northamptonshire Yeomanry had been dogged by misfortune ever since their first actions of the Normandy campaign, and today their troubles were to reach a climax. By sheer bad luck, B Squadron was probing the northern outskirts of Vire as the German column emerged. The Tiger tanks scattered B Squadron's forward Cromwells, which bravely gave battle but as their War Diary related, 'their 75mm guns are no match for the Tiger'. In a further stroke of bad luck, artillery support was withheld to enable a spotting aircraft to direct rocket-armed Typhoons onto the German formation. But the spotting aircraft was shot down and the

2/Northants Yeomanry
final defensive position

la Bistière

The Advance of
the Tigers from
Vire

la Papillonnière

Railway Bridge

VIRE

FOOs were unable to direct the fighter-bombers.

Reaching the road junction at la Papillonnière, the German infantry dismounted to accompany the leading tanks as they attempted to deploy off the main road towards their objective, the high ground around la Bistière at Points 145 and 119 [modern 144 and 127]. Three B Squadron Cromwells were destroyed around la Papillonnière. The outclassed Cromwells slowly withdrew towards la Bistière, where the regiment's headquarters was trying to improvise a roadblock. Then, to their horror, a further Tiger tank appeared behind them on the rising ground 500 metres to the east of the road and proceeded to pick off a further three B Squadron tanks as they fell back.

Reaching la Bistière, the survivors of B Squadron had new hope. Here if anywhere, the Tiger tank might be at a disadvantage, ambush at close range giving even the Cromwell tank's 75mm gun a chance of disabling a Tiger. But hope was short-lived. 'Though the Tigers were engaged at short range, shells from our guns seemed to have little effect.' The leading Tiger was hit at close range as it roared over an open crossroads but escaped damage and, as soon as it could traverse its heavy turret, despatched the ambusher in a ball of flame. One Tiger, SS-*Unterscharführer* Streng's, was indeed immobilised north of la Bistière, though repeated antitank hits succeeded only in giving the crew a fright and damaging a track so that the tank had to be towed to safety.

KG Weiss had stirred a hornets' nest. Instead of uniting with Meindl's paratroops from the west, and still hoping to see *KG* Meyer approaching

The leading Tiger tank was hit as it emerged from behind the white house, by a Cromwell waiting in this side road.

Pz Kpfw MkVIs, Tigers, moving across open country. Two Tiger tanks stood back-to-back above Point 119.

from the east, they found only enemies around la Bistière. Attempts to move off the main highway achieved little as the country lanes proved simply too narrow for the huge tanks, yet unsupported infantry fell into ambushes. The close terrain saved the Cromwells of C Squadron lined up along the Etouvy – la Bistière road. C Squadron remained on the ridge through the day, covering the retreat of the Northants' headquarters from la Bistière. Restricted to the main highway, the heavy Tiger tanks took up defensive positions around la Bistière, two of them pressing forward as far as the slopes above Point 119, and stopping literally back-to-back, guarding the approaches. In fact, they had unwittingly stopped within half a mile of 'Pip' Roberts' 11th Armoured Division tactical headquarters at le Reculey. Later that afternoon, Weiss's *1. Kompanie* of Tiger tanks and Gräbner's *2 PSW Kompanie* of half-tracks moved north west out of Vire on the Torigni road and eventually made contact with forward elements of *3 Fallschirmjägerdivision*.

Battered by attacks from all directions, the Tiger tanks around la Bistière suffered only one loss: Rowsovski's tank, number 233, whose turret was pierced no less than seven times as British guns at close range finally found weak points in its armour. Far worse was the suffering of the Northants Yeomanry. Tank commander Keith Jones recalls:

'Armour-piercing shots were predictably ineffective against Tiger frontal armour, but when they fired at the flanks the solidarity of the bocage walls in which the hedges had been rooted for centuries broke the force of the AP before it even reached the Tigers. This was a day in which failure to equip the regiment with the one-in-four Sherman Fireflies, mounting 17-pounder guns, as accorded to the armoured regiments, made all the

157

11th Armoured HQ at le Reculey

Point 119 is at the bottom of the dip where the road crosses a small stream. The Tiger tanks held the sunlit fields to the west (left of the road), unaware that 'Pip' Roberts' 11th Armoured TAC HQ was just a few fields further north.

difference.'[3]

As well as losing tanks, several headquarters vehicles had been abandoned in la Bistière. In forty-eight hours of combat, forty-seven Cromwell tanks were lost, leaving only a composite squadron of fourteen at the end of the action. Soon after, this proud battalion was disbanded.

NEDFORCE AT LES GRANDS BONFAITS

As promised by Major Robinson, Major Thornburn's infantry company had been reinforced by two platoons of A Company, and two of the 6-pounder guns of the KSLI's own antitank platoon. Further help came in the shape of A Squadron, 3/RTR. And no British defensive position in Normandy would be complete without the presence of the (ubiquitous) Royal Artillery. The Forward Observation Officer present was Captain Peter Garrett of the Ayrshire Yeomanry. In his Sherman tank, Captain Garrett represented the eyes and ears of an entire Field Regiment, RA, with its twenty-four towed 25-pounder guns ready to deliver pre-designated defensive fire missions at a mere moment's notice.

The defensive position (so nearly abandoned the previous evening) appeared almost ideal. Major Thornburn's first priority was visibility: ensuring that his platoons were deployed so as to get the earliest warning of an approaching enemy. From north east to south east, the view extended for all of four hundred metres. The second priority, clear fields of fire for the platoon Bren guns, was not so vital in this instance since artillery would be the primary means of stopping an enemy advancing on the position. Nevertheless, in the last resort the infantry platoons had to be able to support each other with interlocking fields of fire, so the five available rifle platoons were spaced evenly around the position. The riflemen dug-in in open ground, well clear of hedgerows which might attract artillery fire or trees which would cause incoming rounds to airburst (high explosive shells detonating on the ground send fragments upwards rather than down into infantry slit-trenches). Antitank guns were set up in between platoons, away from the riflemen (the gunners with their unwieldy artillery pieces were largely dependent on concealment and had a horror of riflemen giving away their emplacements by milling around near them). Thornburn later reflected 'It was a lovely position.'

However, Thornburn admitted to a 'tragic error of judgement' with regard to the siting of the supporting tanks. A Squadron, 3/RTR, had joined Nedforce as night fell and as normal went into night '*laager*'. In the absence of the squadron commander, the second in command was an old desert hand, and true to his past experience he formed his fifteen tanks nose-to-tail in a circle under the trees in the heart of the position. In the featureless desert, this had been standard procedure. In the rolling countryside of Normandy, experience was to show that tanks were better

Les Grands Bonfaits from the west, behind Ned Thornburn's HQ in the orchard, which was larger in 1944.

dispersed in covering terrain, ideally in hull-down positions in which only their turrets would be visible and exposed to enemy fire. Some of the crews spaced their tanks as best they could, but still they were a dense target.

The morning had dawned bright and clear. The men stood-to and had breakfast. There was even time for a wash and a shave. Furtive movements were observed in the orchards surrounding le Busq, and the sound of distant vehicles carried on the easterly breeze reminded the troops that the enemy was not far off to the west. A few desultory artillery rounds were sent in that direction, and a few German rounds came back – apparently in response but with hindsight more likely ranging rounds in preparation for

The northern slopes of the Nedforce position (looking east to German held Estry).

the German counter attack. Then towards the middle of the day a violent bombardment erupted over the position.

It is a principle of artillery bombardment that a sudden, unexpected burst of extreme ferocity is more effective than a gradual 'softening up'. With no warning, the air above les Grands Bonfaits filled with the shriek of descending mortar bombs. Flashes and blasts of detonating shells were followed by a showers of dirt and stones, of leaves and severed branches. The infantry pressed themselves into the earth at the bottom of their entrenchments. The tank crews were caught outside their tanks, the comparative safety of the armoured vehicles denied them as climbing up to the narrow hatches would mean exposure to a hail of deadly shrapnel.

The bombardment stopped. In the comparative silence, fire crackled, leaves fluttered down, the plaintive cries for stretcher bearers began. Some tanks were in flames, all were more or less damaged, among them the FOO's Sherman. Suddenly, a dozen Panzers were approaching, and enemy infantry could be seen darting from cover to cover as they worked their way forward. The tanks' sensitive '19 set' wirelesses were all either unmanned or inoperable. The FOO, Captain Garrett, shouted to Thornburn in desperation, 'I'm off the air. I can't call for fire.' The only workable 19 set was Thornburn's own, in his unarmoured 15cwt truck. A rough-and-ready relay was quickly established: Garrett shouted fire orders and Thornburn 'repeated some incomprehensible jargon on my blower'. The defensive fire mission came swiftly.

'Sure enough, the D.F. came down, and bang on target. I suppose we had the whole Field Regiment. I was even offered Typhoons, but when I asked what safety margin they required, and was told 400 yards, I dared not accept since the enemy was only 150 yards away at the most.'[4]

The situation remained uncertain. Tank officers informed Thornburn that they would have to abandon the position, though in this situation the infantry commander was technically in command. The decision was resolved by Corporal 'Titch' Hayward of 4/KSLI's antitank platoon, who crawled back from his gun position to declare that his gun had a German tank in its sights and 'If he advances another five yards I've got him in the bag.' Heartened by such determination, the tank men agreed to remain. Having lost his own Sherman Troop leader Sergeant 'Buck' Kite manned the Firefly of the troop which carried a 17-pounder gun in place of the much lower velocity 75mm main armament. This was the only Allied tank gun in Normandy with a chance of penetrating the front armour of a Panther or Tiger, and as such was always picked out by the Panzers as a preferred target. In the close range action that ensued, Kite spotted:

'...the silhouettes of two more Panthers... in the wheat field next to us. The wheat, almost ready for harvesting, was high and each time the enemy fired at us the shells slashed a narrow furrow through the stalks. One of the

Shells slashed narrow furrows through the standing corn.

two tanks was destroyed. Suddenly, I saw the cannon of the other tank...
swing round in our direction. There was nothing I could do but watch the
glint of the approaching shell. I can still see the wheat stalks parted by the
passage of the shell.'

Kite's Firefly was knocked out; he himself was badly wounded, and
wounded again after being carried to the KSLI aid post. The squadron
appealed to their colonel for help and were told to look out for elements of
Guards Armoured somewhere to the north. These were the Irish Guards,
whose Shermans were in the vicinity of la Marvindière, fighting their own
battle and complaining – according to one well-connected officer – that 'no
matter what is said in Parliament, the German guns penetrate our armour,
and our 75mms do not penetrate theirs'.[5] (It was a Guards Armoured
officer, the Conservative member for North Lanark, who had provoked the
Secretary of State for War to deny in Parliament that Allied tanks were
inferior.) Hopes that the Guards might arrive to rescue the beleaguered
3/RTR were not realised.

As quickly as it started, the battle died away. Nedforce stood firm on the
ridgeline. Their stand was rewarded by the Germans' acceptance that the
high ground was too strong to be taken.

GERMAN TACTICS

By 1944, German tactics had evolved to allow for such harsh realities as
shortages of equipment and (particularly) loss of control of the skies.

Nevertheless, certain fundamentals of German battle tactics remained constant. The goal of German doctrine was to encircle and destroy the enemy. The recognised way to achieve this was by outflanking him. Where an enemy line was unbroken, a frontal attack 'Frontalangriff' would be required, focusing all fighting arms on a main point of effort: the 'Schwerpunkt'. By achieving local fire superiority against an enemy weak point, that enemy would be first shocked into inaction by a combination of firepower and surprise, then paralyzed by suppressive fire and smoke until the moment the tank-infantry assault broke over them. Finally, the integrity of the enemy line would be ruptured, permitting infiltration and 'rolling up' of flanks. This was an expensive business, generally the last option of a German commander. Experienced in the more open, mobile war in the east, the Germans looked to infiltrate and outflank the enemy wherever possible.

Nevertheless, it was the tactics of 'Frontalangriff' which were attempted against Ned Thornburn's 4/KSLI at les Grands Bonfaits. The Germans opened with long range antitank fire to draw the fire of the outranged British, and destroy as much supporting armour as possible. With the British antitank capability written-down, German armour closed. Behind a sharp barrage of high explosive and smoke, covered by tanks, the infantry advanced in small groups, bounding forward in short dashes, using natural cover and camouflage. Infantry leaders would work up to and around the enemy, aiming to pick off their officers and panic the defenders with encircling fire. Such tactics often succeeded, but in this case they signally failed. So great was the setback at les Grands Bonfaits that the Germans became convinced that there was no future in attacking there, and thereafter they preferred to infiltrate up the Presles-Burcy valley.

Ned Thornburn reflected with satisfaction that German armour advanced very cautiously, and the infantry appeared unwilling to close on his 4/KSLI position. Other observers record similar feelings. Steel Brownlie noted that German activity throughout much of the BLUECOAT battle was 'usually in platoon strength with a couple of tanks, taking every advantage of the thick country.' Major How of the Herefords went so far as to criticise the German command for wasting their strength by attacking in 'penny packets'. Some British observers even speculated that the German troops opposing them were not of the same calibre as German formations of earlier war years. There is some truth in this. By 3 August, even the SS Panzer divisions were having to accept growing numbers of non-German manpower in their ranks, while the need to husband artillery ammunition and preserve their dwindling numbers of battle tanks was a constant worry. Nevertheless, this is not the full story. While the resolve and tenacity of such British units as Thornburn's Shropshires cannot be questioned, the *Hohenstaufen* too were élite troops. Since June, *Generalinspekteur der*

163

Panzertruppen Heinz Guderian had approved changes in Panzer tactics uniquely tailored to suit the close terrain of the 'invasion front' where it frequently proved impossible to co-ordinate large numbers of tanks. In place of the normal concentrations of armour, the new *Panzertrupptaktik* permitted independent action by units down to the *Zug* (three or four tanks) or even fewer (*Halbzüge*).[6]

Finally, at les Grands Bonfaits and in numerous engagements along the Vire-Vassy road, it was the overwhelming power of the Royal Artillery that made the difference, making massed frontal attacks impossible to sustain and driving the Germans to adopt the tactics of infiltration.

ROYAL ARTILLERY

Time and time again in the Normandy campaign, the gunners tipped the balance. The Royal Artillery emerged from the First World War with a reputation as the most professionally skilled arm of the British Army, and this reputation was to be upheld throughout the 1944-1945 campaign in north west Europe. In 1941, Churchill observed:

'Renown awaits the commander who first, in this war, restores the artillery to its prime position on the battlefield.'[7]

Montgomery was such a commander. Ever a realist, Montgomery played to his army's strengths and to his enemies' weaknesses. He believed that superior German small arms and sophisticated infantry tactics could be overcome by blowing the enemy to bits with high explosive.

The statistics are impressive. Single brigades (of three infantry battalions or tank regiments) were routinely allocated a full Field Regiment, RA, a unit whose twenty-four field guns could deliver up to 1,800 rounds in fifteen minutes. Good logistical systems existed to support such rates of fire, and the response to calls for pre-planned defensive fire could be measured in minutes if not seconds. More than one German POW is reported to have asked for 'a look at one of your wonderful automatic field guns'. German battle reports likened British barrages to those of the

25-pounder field guns of the Ayrshire Yeomanry advancing from Dickie's Bridge towards le Bény Bocage.

First World War: one *Hohenstaufen* officer's reaction was to quote Dante's *Inferno*: '...abandon hope all ye who enter here!'

The guns supporting Nedforce in the battle for les Grands Bonfaits were closer than usual to the action. Little more than a mile to the west of Major Thornburn's strongpoint was the defensive 'box' of 4/KSLI, containing B and C Companies, plus Support Company's Carrier and Mortar Platoons, also providing safe haven for the headquarters of 3/RTR. And a further mile west was another box: on the Burcy ridge, between the hamlets of Forgues and les Grippes, was the defensive box of the 1/Herefords, sheltering the headquarters of Brigadier Churcher's 159 Brigade. Also in this box, unusually far forward, were the towed field guns of the Ayrshire Yeomanry. Feeling exposed in the rear areas, with German units infiltrating from east to west, the field regiment chose – exceptionally – to close up with the front line infantry. The wisdom of this move was soon to become clear. At one point, as the Ayrshires' regimental headquarters staff busied themselves over their radio sets, the unflappable Lance Bombadier Burton quietly entered the pig sty that doubled as RHQ, bearing a tray of cocoa for the officers. Setting the tray down, he murmured in a confidential tone, 'Excuse me, sir, it is reported that a German patrol is coming up through the wood behind. Thank you, sir', then slipped out as quietly as he had entered.[8]

The division's other field regiment, the 'Sexton' self-propelled guns of 13/Royal Horse Artillery, had already encountered the enemy. On approaching their firing positions near le Désert, an area supposed to have been cleared, they had come under direct antitank fire. Their movement became even brisker. Patrick Delaforce recalls:

> '...the immense thrill for a young, green twenty year old of leading a troop of four huge Sexton 25 pounders under fire; on the move at thirty miles per hour the radio ordered "Action!" and we burst straight off the road through hedges to get into action. We had shells in the air within a minute – RHA tradition!'

The 13/RHA War Diary paints a vivid picture of the situation around le Désert on 3 August:

> 'Our own guns maintained a notable accuracy and retained the confidence and later the great appreciation of the Bde. This was the first day of persistent infiltration and counter-attacks, and the first of the days when the CO was continuously on his wireless with the exception of only a few hrs, varying between two and four, of sleep. The guns were engaging targets almost without pause as is evidenced by the fact that all bty were most reluctant to remain loaded because their pieces were so hot.'

(The regiment experienced the unsettling event of a Sexton blowing up when its 25-pounder gun malfunctioned.)

> 'Added complications were the very unusual danger to the guns posns

Sextons of 13/RHA, 11th Armoured division's self-propelled field regiment.

from inf and tks who were swanning about in the area, being at one stage within two hundred yds. H Bty came out of action and assumed an ATk role: the AA Crusaders (antiaircraft tanks mounting twin Oerlikon 20mm guns) joined the fray. The same thing happened the next day... It was really wonderful that in spite of these distractions the response from the guns remained so quick and accurate and steady.'

Patrick Delaforce, recalls:

'At dusk during BLUECOAT, I personally laid out several hundred yards – overlapping – of trip wire with flares, a hundred yards in front of our gun positions. Though we had the very capable 8/Rifle Brigade in front, we took no chances against infiltration. At night, a dozen SOS targets would be requested on cross roads and other forming up points. So if the infantry or our FOO said over the radio "SOS on FERGUSON, scale five", some Panzer Grenadiers' night manouvre would be rudely disturbed!'

Not far away from le Désert, the self-propelled artillery regiment of Guards Armoured Division had an even closer encounter. The Sextons of 153/Field Regiment, the Leicester Yeomanry, had advanced through the night from just south of St-Martin-des-Besaces to Point 176 [modern 177]. The unit war diary records that 'The location of our forward troops was uncertain but Division were of the opinion that the area was safe'. Division were wrong. By 09.00 hours, the gun lines were formed and the Leicester Yeomanry commenced firing in support of the Irish Guards holding la Marvindière. As a precaution, the battery captains sent reconnaissance patrols out to the flanks and forward of the undefended position. These ran into a 9 *SS Panzerdivision* raiding party. For twenty minutes, confusion reigned and there was a real risk of the whole regiment being overrun. Fire missions

were abandoned and Sextons fired over open sights at enemy tanks and *Panzergrenadiere* emerging from trees barely one hundred metres away. Armour piercing rounds were seen to bounce off the front armour of the Panther tanks. When these were exhausted the gunners carried on with high explosive, virtually useless against the tanks, but when fired into the trees the airburst proved effective against the enemy infantry. Some guns even used up their last HE and fired smoke rounds before breaking off the action. Meanwhile, officers tried to supervise an orderly withdrawal, though the exits from the fields were narrow and covered by enemy fire. In at least one case, a Sexton was driven off the field by a gunner who had never before driven a vehicle. Though personnel losses were mercifully light, the toll of lost equipment was heavy. It would have been heavier still but for the timely appearance of 17-pounder-armed M10 tank destroyers of 21/Anti-Tank Regiment. One of these M10s, Sergeant Farrow's, fired three 17-pounder rounds through the stone walls of a cow byre; next day he found that they had indeed blown up a Panther. The Yeomanry lost four Sextons and two officers' Sherman tanks, together with twenty-two other vehicles. By early evening, the survivors resumed firing from the ground they had occupied before their move south.[9]

THE INFILTRATORS

The Germans' adoption of 'marauding' tactics effectively threatened the entire battle zone. Infantry units of platoon strength backed up by a small number of tanks might be encountered anywhere to the rear of 11th Armoured Division. Early in the day, enemy forces moved westwards behind the 23/Hussars and 8/Rifle Brigade position, their approach up the valley screened from view by a fold in the ground. The failure to hold les

167

Moulins had left a blind spot which the Germans, forestalled at les Grands Bonfaits, were quick to exploit. By 10.00 hours Presles was once again in German hands: 'A very annoying thing,' 'Pip' Roberts recorded. The 23/Hussars - 8/RB group on the hill at le Bas Perrier was now not only cut off, but exposed on a slope facing the new enemy threat. One squadron of tanks after another fell under direct enemy fire, fire which the majority of the Shermans with their 75mm guns saw no point in returning.

News that Germans had penetrated as far as the artillery lines around Point 176 perturbed VIII Corps headquarters. As fighting intensified on the very doorstep of 11th Armoured Division's tactical headquarters at le Reculey, le Beny-Bocage appeared under threat from the east. Along the British 'front' (still more a series of outposts than any sort of continuous line), nightfall brought little respite. At la Bistière, the Northants Yeomanry lost a further eight of their Cromwell tanks, destroyed in dispersed leaguers by infiltrating German patrols. Their burnt-out remains were found next morning, in some cases surrounded by the contents of the survivors' pockets, emptied before they were marched into captivity. The fortified 'hedgehog' defences of 159 Brigade above Burcy and of 29 Brigade above Presles were not directly threatened. The outposts of Fife and Forfars and Monmouths at Pavée and of Hussars and Rifles at le Bas Perrier survived, pounded by the enemy, at times cut off, but with steady support from the guns of the Royal Artillery. The beleaguered Guardsmen at la Marvindière stood their ground even without the looked-for support of their artillery. Their situation was grim, though shortly to improve. The British front held.

Reference

1 *Safely Home*, W Steel Brownlie, p 28.

2 Meyer, p 164.

3 *Sixty-Four Days of a Normandy Summer: With a Tank Unit Until After D-Day*, Keith Jones, 1990, ISBN 0-7090-4240-X, p 152.

5 Verney, p 172.

6 *Panzertruppen volume 2*, Thomas L Jentz, p 182.

7 Quoted in Graham, p 133.

8 *The Proud Trooper*, W Steel Brownlie, 1964, p 385.

9 *153rd Leicestershire Yeomanry Field Regiment, RA, TA, 1939-1945*, Winslow and Brassey, 1947, p 18-23.

SS troops advancing through corn.

CHAPTER EIGHT

Friday 4 to Sunday 6 August –
THE LINE HOLDS

THE LINES ARE DRAWN

The opposing sides had very different views of the battle they were fighting. On the British side, VIII Corps believed they had created a deep salient which they were determined to hold until XXX Corps to the east could advance alongside. Von Kluge, however, remained convinced that the true front line was still far to the north of the current action, and that the British 'breakthrough' amounted only to pockets of resistance capable of being isolated and overrun.

The two high commands also differed in the importance they attached to this sector. For Montgomery, the primary objective of BLUECOAT had been achieved. With new leadership in place in XXX Corps, his attention moved to the eastern end of the battle zone where Operation TOTALIZE, the Canadian drive on Falaise, was due to begin on 8 August. Like Eisenhower, Montgomery had advance warning from ULTRA decrypts of an enemy buildup presaging an offensive towards Avranches. But it was agreed that no specific action was needed for what would probably be a German disaster.

Von Kluge meanwhile had a strong personal interest in stabilising the situation north of Vire. His absolute imperative was to be seen to be putting divisions in place for the *Führer's* offensive. Reports reaching his headquarters the previous day had spoken of breakthroughs and isolated British units in the VIII Corps sector. Could Kluge strip forces from here too? Early on 4 August, Kluge checked with *II SS Panzer Korps* that *Aufklärungsgruppe* Olboeter was in place on the Vire-Vassy road. It was, having arrived in the combat area evening 3 August. So was *Heerespionierbattaillon 600*, whose pioneers had already stiffened the defences around Chênedollé. And was the road absolutely clear? The answer came back. The road was still being disputed west of Viessoix. The British breakout had still not been contained and yet more force wanted for Mortain would have to be sent to Vire. There could be no question of disengaging the *Hohenstaufen*.

From this point on, the outcome of Operation BLUECOAT would be decided not by brilliant manoeuvre but by grit, grim determination, and speed of reinforcement. And up to this point, the Germans had succeeded in reinforcing failure faster that British had reinforced their success. The speed with which *9 SS Panzerdivision* had been moved to the area of crisis

169

demonstrated a clear awareness by the high command of the importance of the sector. By contrast, perilous gaps had been allowed to open to the rear of 11th Armoured Division, creating a virtual no man's land behind the British front line. With boldness bordering on recklessness, 11th Armoured had resisted sending units back from the front to secure lines of communication. Now, at last, reinforcements were arriving to fill the void.

REINFORCEMENTS

In the knowledge that 3rd Infantry Division was available to support 11th Armoured, the infantry of 15th Scottish could now turn to assist Guards Armoured. All through 3 August, the Scots had pushed eastwards along the Arclais ridge, north of the Rubec valley. Most of their supporting armour bogged in the Rubec valley, but the infantry pressed on and by 22.30 hours, elements of 6/Royal Scots Fusiliers at last came in sight of Montchauvet. Early on 4 August, 44 Brigade's other two battalions,

N

Grenadier Guards Churchills run through 'mortar gulch' south of Cathéolles.

The same place in 2002. All the houses have been demolished to make way for the widened D577 Vire to Villers-Bocage road.

8/Royal Scots and 6/King's Own Scottish Borderers, tackled the ridge south of the Rubec. This was a daunting obstacle: a near-perpendicular bluff impassable even to carriers. But at last this ridge too was swept clear. The road to Montchauvet was open, 'Mortar Gulch' was no longer under enemy observation, and Guards Armoured Division could swing south and east to shore up the VIII Corps' left flank. First Montchauvet, then Montchamp fell, following misunderstandings between *9 SS Panzerdivision* and the remnants of *21 Panzer*. The door briefly appeared open for the Guards to fight their way through to relieve their three forward battalions, still cut off at la Marvindière. But during the night violent German counter attacks recovered the lost ground.

Meanwhile, as 3rd Division's 185 Brigade was rushed to the front, its leading battalions were directed at 11th Armoured Division's greatest areas of concern. 2/KSLI ran straight into the armoured battlegroup marauding around Point 176 and suffered heavy casualties. The 2/Warwicks struggled forward past Point 176, encountering groups of Germans as they made their way to the Estry ridge, and finally re-took Presles in a midnight attack. By noon on 4 August, the road to le Bas Perrier was open and first along it were a column of ambulances full of 23/Hussars and 8/RB casualties. The Royal Norfolks passed through 'Pip' Roberts' tactical headquarters at le Reculey and at first light attacked la Bistière (where in desperation for lack of infantry some Cromwell crews had actually dismounted to reconnoitre on foot). Lacking information about the enemy, the Norfolks pushed two companies straight down the road. Confused fighting raged in la Bistière throughout the day.

THE TURNING TIDE

The *Hohenstaufen* plan for 4 August was a simple continuation of the previous day's offensive. With armour and infantry groups still operating behind the forward British outposts, *9 SS Panzerdivision* was to be the hammer striking the anvil of the Tiger tanks at la Bistière. Panther tanks and Panzer grenadiers continued to press westwards, aiming to cut the Vire-Villers Bocage highway and establish a line from Beaulieu and la Ferronnière in the east to la Graverie in the west, where it was hoped a firm union with Meindl's paratroops could be forged. Steadily, the strength of the mighty *Hohenstaufen* was being reduced. By the end of 4 August, two days of continuous fighting had cost nearly half the division's tanks, with only eight *Sturmgeschütze*, eight Panzer IV, and eighteen Panther tanks remaining operational. Losses of this magnitude could not be sustained. And all the time the British seemed to be growing stronger, with the risk of the encircling German forces themselves being encircled and cut off.

In the afternoon of 4 August, von Kluge was dismayed to learn from Eberbach that the British were still on the Vire-Vassy road. Earlier

171

Kluge and Eberbach debate sending the *Frundsberg*.

optimism that a new line had been formed between Estry, Burcy, and la Bistière faded (these areas were indeed occupied by German forces but in no sense was there a line). Worse news was to follow. Eberbach was still unable to confirm that his forces were in contact with *Seventh Army* to the west. Unpalatable and momentous decisions would have to be made. This resulted in the *Hohenstaufen's* sister division, *10 SS Panzerdivision 'Frundsberg'*, being pulled out of the line and moved south from Aunay to Vassy. At least Kluge could argue that he was moving the *Frundsberg* closer to the start line of the *Führer's* planned offensive.

Weiss's Tigers fought on at la Bistière, those around Point 119 frequently becoming surrounded. Finally, around 22.30 hours on 4 August came orders to withdraw. Weiss pulled back to Vire. The pincer movement intended to cut off the forward elements of 11th Armoured Division had been abandoned, and with its abandonment came the acceptance of that a British breakout had truly occurred. There could no longer be any hope of restoring the German line to the Souleuvre valley. Indeed, American pressure on Vire was building from the west, and Meindl's parachute infantry were clinging grimly to the ruins of the town. The Tiger tanks did not dwell there long, leaving before daybreak on 5 August on a roundabout route that led them back to Chênedollé.

THE ORDEAL ON PERRIER RIDGE

On the afternoon of 4 August, the reinforcement of le Bas Perrier by 2/Warwicks had come just in time. As the leading company arrived to relieve 8/Rifle Brigade, the observation post on the crest of the ridge at Hill 242 [modern 243] was already reporting enemy movement. Soon, brief glimpses of enemy infantry darting from cover to cover were seen on the ridge. As the Warwicks settled into their positions, the Germans gained possession of Hill 242 and reinforced their position in Chênedollé.

By 5 August, von Kluge was resigned to the necessity of forming a new defensive line, just north of the Vire-Vassy road. But keeping that road open was still a priority. And right in the centre of the newly-drawn line, between the German bulwarks of Estry in the east and Vire in the west, was the British position on the high ground south of Presles: the Perrier ridge. This salient was a clear threat to the vital road. It had to be taken. The whole of Bittrich's *II SS Panzer Korps* would be used. *9 SS Panzerdivision* was already regrouping around the ridge; *10 SS Panzer* was on its way. Both would be used to crush the British position. In fact, *10 SS Panzerdivision* was having great difficulty making the move. Disengaging from their fight with XXX Corps was not easy; and their passage westwards to Vassy was fraught with difficulty due to an increasing torrent of supply and medical vehicles now flowing eastwards along the narrow roads.

Ordered to begin the process of straightening the line, *9 SS Panzerdivision* attacked on the evening of 5 August. Up to then, the day had been relatively quiet for the Warwicks infantry and 23/Hussars at le Bas Perrier. True, one of Weiss' Tiger tanks had worked its way up onto the ridge above, at le Haut Perrier, but the Hussars' Shermans were by now well concealed. The Tiger had contented itself with putting three shells through a Household Cavalry scout car, and later a self propelled M10 antitank gun of the Royal Artillery. The Hussars' historian recalled that 'It really began to look as though the 9 SS *Panzerdivision* had had about enough.' VIII Corps felt the time was right to begin disengaging 11th Armoured Division in preparation for a chase should the German line crumble, and the Northants. Yeomanry was already being withdrawn. British hopes were premature. *Hohenstaufen* had taken a terrible beating. Some of its units had narrowly escaped encirclement in the British rear areas and needed time to reorganise. Nevertheless, another attack was being prepared.

The storm broke suddenly. A concentration of *Nebelwerfer* rockets fell on le Bas Perrier, temporarily paralysing the Warwicks' battalion command post. Once again, infantry and Sherman tanks fought a close range battle with the Germans who had survived the hail of artillery as they climbed the ridge. An infantryman recalls the noise and confusion:

> 'We could see nothing. Suddenly the hedge was parted violently just to our right and a Sherman tank broke through, reversing slowly, firing non-stop at some invisible enemy. There was small arms fire now on all sides: our shells were still screeching past just overhead; there were loud explosions and the roar of the tank engine grew louder... German infantry must be very close... There was a loud explosion from the Sherman tank. A cloud of dust rose into the air. The crew threw themselves out of the hatches

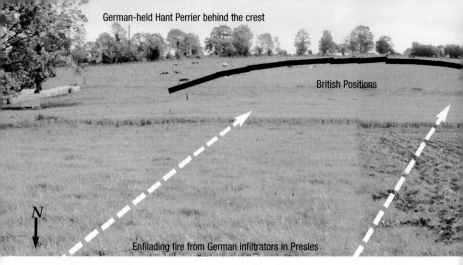

German-held Hant Perrier behind the crest

British Positions

N

Enfilading fire from German infiltrators in Presles

On these slopes to the west of le Bas Parrier, opposite Presles to the north, was the main position of 23/Hussars throughout the battle.

and ran crouching towards us.'

And so it went on. Lasting well into the night, the fight was resumed in the morning of 6 August, this time with *10 SS Panzerdivision* leading the assault. But with the constant support of the British artillery, the position still held.

THE 'NOR-MONS' AT PAVÉE

Throughout 5 August, 3rd Division's reinforcement of the forward British units continued. 185 Brigade pushed on south towards the Vire-Vassy road and, towards evening, its 1/Royal Norfolks were assigned to go to the aid of 11th Armoured Division's 3/Monmouths, still beleaguered at Pavée. The Norfolks' Major Humphrey Wilson gives a vivid description of the scene he found on reaching the 159 Brigade headquarters at Burcy:

'Around midnight I made contact with Brigadier Jack Churcher who pointed out a burning ridge in the distance and said "There are the Monmouths, or what is left of them. Be careful how you go as we are only in wireless touch with them. Be prepared to take over from them at first light".'

Churcher was not exaggerating the plight of the Monmouths. On his arrival, Wilson found the Monmouths' hilltop at Pavée under continual bombardment. The men were exhausted. Virtually cut off from brigade headquarters, they were improvising great cider barrels as shelters for their more seriously wounded. Their CO, Lieutenant Colonel Hubert Orr was no less exhausted than his men, but determined that withdrawal could not take place in daylight. Besides, he pointed out, 'If the Germans are so anxious to have Pavée then we had better stay here.'

So it was to be. The morning mist burned off to find the Norfolks'

leading B Company exposed on a hillside north of Pavée, where it was promptly pounded by German mortars. A and C Companies tried different routes, but all suffered casualties. By nightfall the combined numbers of the two infantry regiments barely totalled 550. With increased shelling heralding a new enemy attack, and withdrawal problematic, the two battalion commanders agreed to stay and pool their forces into a single unit, under Orr. A battlegroup of 'Nor-Mons' was formed.

With enemy tanks and infantry closing on the beleaguered hilltop, the sole remaining artillery FOO, Major Mitchell of the Ayrshire Yeomanry, single-handedly managed observation posts covering all angles of attack, tirelessly directing defensive fire in all directions. Brigade offered fighter bombers. But the Germans were so close that the red smoke marking the

The small village of Burcy, viewed from le Bas Perrier. The road cutting diagonally up the hill north of Burcy leads to the 159 Brigade position just north of the ridge.

enemy drifted back over the Nor-Mons, and from the cloudless blue sky American Thunderbolts set about bombing the British position. Major How of the Herefords recalled, 'With so much shelling and so many "Moaning Minnies" it didn't seem to make much difference'.[1] Two miles back, Mitchell's own Ayrshire Yeomanry fired their 25-pounder field guns until the barrels were red hot, expending 250 rounds per gun in the action. By 21.00 hours, the Ayrshires' ammunition was running out. Were the lines of supply broken? At the last minute, a column of thirty RASC trucks was spotted. The Yeomen cheered them up the hill, then resumed firing for a further two hours.

Patrick Delaforce's Royal Horse Artillery added their fire:

'I remember the awful feeling of horror and helplessness as the poor, wretched Mons got stonked out of their lives a few hundred yards in front. The noisy, mobile, efficient "Moaning Minnies" needed fantastic FOO skill to track them down and shell them into silence.'

German mortars are generally accepted to have caused up to seventy per cent of Allied casualties in Normandy. The 'Moaning Minnie' rockets ('Screaming Meemies' to the Americans) fired by the *Nebelwerfer* launchers arrived with a sound which has been likened to underground train, inflicting psychological damage in addition to physical casualties. But the Forward Observers did their job. Unlike their American and German counterparts, British battery commanders were typically not with the guns but forward with the units they supported. And once spotted, each German artillery position was subjected to counter-battery fire averaging twenty tons of shells.[2]

The road running north from the memorials through Pavée to la Fauvellière. This was the high water mark of the *Frundsberg* assault.

German fire came in from east, south, and west. German tanks (inevitably called 'Tigers' by the British, though mainly Panzer IVs of *2/10. SS-Panzer Regiment*) plunged into the British positions. So many of the Fife and Forfars' Shermans were destroyed that after disengaging to rearm, one squadron was disbanded. The Fifes returned about 19.30 hours to reinvigorate the 'Nor-Mons' at the height of the struggle. Waves of *Frundsberg Panzergrenadiere* came up the hillsides, advancing in short rushes from cover to cover. Outflanking the western side of the positions, they penetrated as far as the little village of la Fauvellière on Hill 224, actually behind the 'Nor-Mons' command post. As the Norfolks' B Company was about to be overrun, Corporal Bates on the extreme right flank seized the section Bren gun from its wounded operator. Firing the blood soaked gun from the hip, he cut down the leading dozen Grenadiers, causing those behind to pause. Hit twice, he fell, recovered his weapon, and continued emptying magazines against the enemy until he was felled by a third, mortal wound from a mortar bomb. The position was held. Sidney 'Basher' Bates died two days later and was posthumously awarded the Victoria Cross.

Corporal Sidney Bates VC.

Meanwhile, Major Mitchell had lost one radio and two of his Gunners, killed at his side. Still he directed the fire. Leaving his command post to assist the Fife and Forfar Shermans on the eastern slope, Mitchell realised that his 25-pounders were ineffective against the Tiger tanks on Hill 242 around le Haut Perrier. He called on the medium artillery with their 4.5 and 5.5 inch guns. 'Splendid laying resulted in an almost direct hit. For a time nothing more was heard, and one eventually withdrew.' If the Tigers could not be penetrated, they could at least be stunned into submission. And the field artillery continued to wreak carnage, entire sections of *Panzergrenadiere* being wiped out on the slopes below Pavée.

Viewed from the German side, the situation of *10 SS Panzerdivision* was becoming desperate. Two days previously, the *Frundsberg* had succeeded in executing that most difficult of actions: a disengagement in front of an advancing enemy. But the orders now given to SS *Oberführer* Harmel were unachievable. His division was to advance south west in readiness for the planned Mortain offensive, yet somehow it was also to serve as a 'reserve' to stabilise the position east of Vire. Far from acting as a 'reserve', the division was ready for action around Viessoix by the afternoon of 6 August, a day late, and was immediately flung against the Pavée position. Its objective was Point 224 [a spot height not indicated on modern maps, but actually the hamlet of la Fauvelliere, inaccurately referred to by the British as Sourdeval]. The fighting was bitter. Towards the end of 6 August, a series of reports from Bittrich's *II SS Panzer Korps* to the headquarters of Eberbach at *5 Panzer-Armee* (the newly renamed *Panzergruppe West)* reveal the awful truth.

At 20.00 hours, Bittrich was upbeat. The attack begun at 17.00 hours had progressed well and *10 SS Panzerdivision* held Hill 224. At 22.45 hours, Hill 224 had been lost, and could be not retaken with the available infantry. This was a bitter blow for Harmel and Bittrich alike; only after desperate attempts to change the situation would such a confession of failure have been sent up the line. Consternation erupted at Eberbach's headquarters. But at 23.00 hours came further bad news: *Frundsberg* had suffered 'important losses'. Even were another battalion of Grenadiers immediately available, they could not prevail. And at 23.40 hours came the final report that *10 SS Panzerdivision* had been pushed back and now had only five tanks operational. Neither *Hohenstaufen* nor, now, *Frundsberg* was going to be joining Hitler's Mortain offensive.

Reference

1 How, p 197.
2 French, p 256.

178

CHAPTER NINE

AFTERMATH AND ASSESSMENT

The German counteroffensive was launched on the night of 6-7 August, greatly under strength. As preparations were completed, von Kluge despaired. But his commanders persuaded him that it was too late to change the plan and that this opportunity to take the initiative, however uncertain of success, would not occur again. Mere hours before the start and far too late for any changes, Hitler intervened suggesting a postponement, offering Kluge further Panzer forces presently east of Paris. Only reluctantly did Hitler yield to Kluge's pleas to continue as planned.

The weather on 7 August was fine. Once the predicted fog cleared, the sky belonged to the 2nd Tactical Air Force. The United States Official History records:

> 'The forward motion of the Mortain counterattack had come to a halt soon after daylight on 7 August, when the Germans drove their tanks off the roads into the fields and hastily threw camouflage nets over them to escape detection.'

Also:

> 'The reaction to the counterattack demonstrated a flexibility and a rapidity of reflex that was most clearly illustrated by the fact that British planes operated effectively on the American front.'[1]

What the writer did not realise (in 1960) was that this effectiveness was also the result of advance preparations based on ULTRA decrypts.[2]

Crewman from a Panther scans the skies for Allied fighter-bombers during the fighting in Normandy, August 1944.

Americans breakthrough in Normandy.

As early as the afternoon of 7 August, Kluge recognised that the attack had failed, and began preparing for the inevitable retreat. Hitler continued to demand single-minded focus on victory, insisting that *9 SS* and *10 SS, Panzerdivisions* along with the *21 Panzerdivision* be thrown in to the fray. Ironically, had *10 SS Panzerdivision* been available, it was to have attacked a lightly defended sector. Had all three German divisions been able to take up their planned positions, the outcome might have been different. But they were not. All were, for the time being, more or less worn out and all were still in the British sector.

The Americans finally secured the rubble that had been Vire, suffering over three thousand casualties. The British 3rd Division advanced to overlook the north side of the Vire-Vassy road. Guards Armoured Division relieved first the three battalions of their comrades grimly holding la Marvindière, then went on to relieve 11th Armoured Division in its positions from Presles to Pavée. On 8 August, Montgomery launched Operation TOTALIZE from Caen towards Falaise, while Patton's 3rd Army continued its run around the German left.

The breakthrough had become breakout. The next step was encirclement at Falaise and the drive to the Seine.

180

BATTLEFIELD TOURS
AND GENERAL NOTES FOR VISITORS

This 'battlefield' bears few remaining signs of war. From Caumont to Vire, only the occasional monument gives a clue to the fighting that took place in 1944. Why visit? If you have any interest in the subject, whether you are engaged in serious research or simply 'passing through', there are rewards.

No matter how many accounts you read, or how good your map reading is, there are always surprises. In the BLUECOAT area, the most frequent surprise is just how little you can see from a given spot. Even today, small, hedgerow-lined fields and rolling ground limit lines-of-sight (or lines-of-fire!). And yet... there are points in this area from which you can see virtually the whole tableau spread out before you. Visiting the key places in this story will add an extra dimension to your understanding, as well as imprinting them on your memory.

The 1:25,000 maps produced by the IGN (*Institut Geographique National*) in the 'Série bleu' are invaluable guides. Fortunately, the entire area is covered by just two: 1413 E 'CAUMONT-L'EVENTE' and 1414 E 'VIRE'.

The two towns, Caumont and Vire, have little to offer in terms of military history. For the visitor in a hurry, St-Martin-des-Besaces at the epicentre of the battlefield has an excellent *Musée de la Percée* well worth the hour's visit (incidentally with a very well stocked bookshop). The museum is open all days except Tuesday, 1 June to 15 September, and closes between 12.00 and 14.00 hours (allow one hour for the tour).

Given the scale of the battle area and the excellence of road links, no specific recommendations are made with regard to accommodation. Small hotels and 'Chambres d'Hôtes' abound, and an Internet search for 'Vire Normandy' will produce ample listings of accommodation.

For those unaccustomed to driving on the right, country lanes empty of traffic can be a real risk when starting off after a brief stop. Try to find some way of reminding yourself which side of the road to use. Even if it means a note on the dashboard, swallow your pride! And even the most experienced right-hand-driver may forget to look the correct way when crossing a road on foot. Take your time and take care.

Finally, this book has done most of the detective work involved in locating battle sites. But if you wish to gain access to farmers' fields (which will usually mean crossing some form of barrier), please introduce yourself first. Now that most French farmers have no personal memories of the war, they are sometimes ignorant of the details of what happened on their land in 1944, and so unaware of the interest their farm may hold for visitors. A few polite words in French almost always lead to open access.

The following recommended routes can be followed either individually, or all together as a single comprehensive tour of the BLUECOAT battlefields.

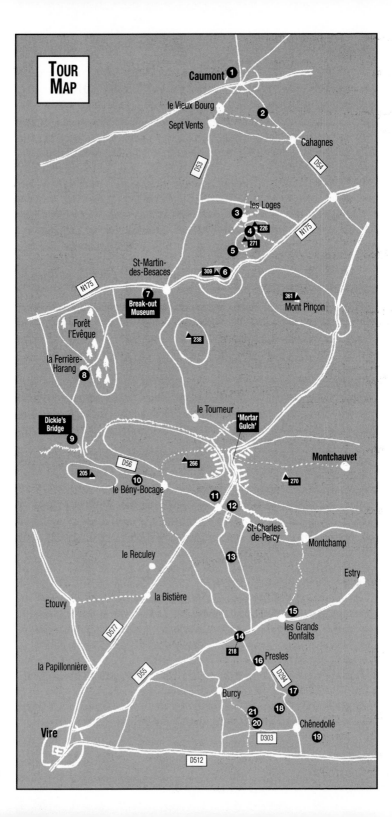

TOUR 1
The Breakout South of Caumont

We start in the centre of Caumont **[1]**, where there is ample car parking. The *Syndicat d'Initiatives* is on the first floor of the Hôtel de Ville, and clean public toilets can be found on the ground floor of the same building.

Set off on the D54, south east in the **direction of Cahagnes**. Following the route of the Grenadier Guards' Churchill tanks, the road descends from the Caumont ridge, with views to the right of the high ground in the distance which was the objective on 30 July. **1.5km** (0.9 miles) **out of Caumont,** there is a monument on the right hand side, and a little lane you can park in while visiting the grave of Lieutenant James Marshall-Cornwall **[2]**. The little copse behind the site is part of what was the Bois de Bavent, referred to by the British (and in this text) as the Lutain Wood.

Moving on south, after another 1.5km (0.9 miles) a small country lane crosses the road. If you do not mind driving on a rough (and possibly muddy) track, **turn right here and drive 3km (1.8 miles)** due west to **le Vieux Bourg**. To the north there are very good views of Caumont and the whole Lutain Wood battle area. **Reaching le Vieux Bourg, turn left towards Sept Vents**, now following the route of the 9/Cameronians. If you decide against the track, simply drive on a short way **into Cahagnes and take the right hand turn onto the Sept-Vents road** (the D193). On the way to Sept Vents, you will pass Ecorigny, where the 2/Argylls halted to regroup along the road.

From Sept Vents, **drive south** on the **D53** for **2.5km** (1.6 miles) **then turn left onto the D107** by a small Calvary. Just **1200m** (0.7 miles) on, **turn right** at a small crossroads (unmarked in 2002) towards les Loges; if you miss this turning, simply continue a further 1200m to meet the D292 at le Chêne Rost and **turn right** here for **Les Loges**.

Arriving in les Loges, pause by the Hôtel de Ville **[3]**. To the north of the road is the area the 2/Argylls' Headquarters Company reached on 30 July. To the south, opposite the Hôtel de Ville, is the track up which some of the Scots Guards Churchills climbed up Hill 226, and after them, Ron Lomas' 6-pounder gun. You can explore this track, but half way to the summit of Hill 226 you will encounter the impassable barrier of the dual carriageway A 84 Autoroute which now cuts the northern slopes of Hill 226. To reach the top, you will need to drive on **through les Loges,** over the bridge spanning the Autoroute, then **turn sharp left** by the picnic area. **500m** (0.3 miles) from this turning, **stop opposite** the farm on your right **[4].** The farm track on your left leads directly to the rock-strewn summit of Hill 226.

Continuing east along this country lane, you pass Fumichon where the *Jagdpanther* disappeared from British view, and **proceed eastwards** along their likely return route to their headquarters at St-Pierre-du-Fresne. Be thankful that you do not have to keep a watch for low-flying 'Jabos'. **Reaching the major N175, turn right towards St-Martin-des-Besaces.** This road runs dead-straight for 2km (1.2 miles), then after a further 500m there is a farm track on the right. If you have time, **turn into this track leading to le Garretière [5]**. This is private property. But if you are willing to ask permission of the farmer, leave your car by the farm, and **walk a further 500m**, you will reach the summit of Hill 280 [the northerly of the two modern hills 271]. This summit, taken by the 6/KOSB on 1 August, offers superb views over Hill 226 (north east), the approaches to Hill 309 (west), and the forbidding mass of the Bois du Homme (nowadays 'Bois de Brimbois') to the south.

Rejoining the main road, continue south west, climbing up to the southern slopes of Hill 309, where you will pass the Coldstream Hill monument on your right **[6]**. Descend into St-Martin-des-Besaces, and the Breakout museum (*Musée de la Percée du Bocage*) is on the left hand side of the road on the far side of the small town **[7]**.

Tour 2
St Martin Des Besaces to Dickie's Bridge

Leaving the Breakout museum, **turn west along the N175**. This stretch of road, and the parallel railway to the north (now the A84 Autoroute) proved particularly difficult for tanks of the 2/Northants Yeomanry to cross. The road runs straight for 2km [1.2 miles], then bends slightly left. 500m after this bend, **take a left turn at a crossroads by a restaurant.** You are now following Dickie Powle's route to the Souleuvre bridge. Just over a kilometre along this road (0.7 miles), **turn right at a crossroads** onto the D185 towards la Ferrière-Harang, 2km distant. Soon, you enter the Forêt l'Evêque: the woods are not so thick nowadays, and the road is now wider and metalled.

The arrival of your car in la Ferrière **[8]** may not receive quite the same ecstatic welcome that greeted the Northants Yeomanry Cromwells. Never mind this, keep to the right, passing the church on your left. **After 1km** (0.6 miles)**, turn left onto the D56,** and after about 2.5km (1.5 miles) you will turn a corner to see the Souleuvre valley before you, the road ahead following a narrow causeway over the flood plain to the famous bridge **[9]**.

If by this stage you are tiring of military history, you may seek stimulation nearby where the partially dismantled span of Gustave Eiffel's 1889 railway bridge, towering above the deep valley, has been turned into a bungee jumping centre.

Alternatively, after enjoying the tranquility of the Souleuvre bridge, you may press on the short distance along the road followed by 23/Hussars into le Bény-Bocage **[10]**. After le Bény-Bocage, **continue east along the D56** to the major D577 highway. You have reached Objective COVENTRY **[11]**. Here, you may **turn left** to return to St Martin through 'Mortar Gulch' and retracing the advance of the Guards through le Tourneur. Or, you may continue the tour across the highway and a further 600m along the D56 to the British cemetery at **St-Charles-de-Percy.**

184

TOUR 3
The Battle of Perrier Ridge

The cemetery at Saint-Charles-de-Percy **[12]** is well worth a visit. Typical of cemeteries constructed and maintained by the War Graves Commission, this is an oasis of dignified tranquillity in which visitors may pause to reflect on sacrifices made a half-century ago. To the north looms the dark massif of Hill 270, still in German hands when the first Cromwell tanks of the Welsh Guards passed this way.

From the cemetery, continue westward for **1km along the D56 into St-Charles-de-Percy. Turn right after the Church,** opposite the Château. **After 1.5km** (0.9 miles), la Crière farm is on your right **[13]**. If you wish to visit the fields where the Leicester Yeomanry's Sextons encountered the *Hohenstaufen*, ask permission at the farmhouse (and be prepared to encounter not Panther tanks, but inquisitive bulls).

2.9km (1.8 miles) further south, you reach a **T junction with the D55.** This is Objective WARWICK, the Vire-Estry road.

Just a few metres **to the west,** by a Calvary, is the crossroads where Sergeant Jones of the 23/Hussars had to juggle radio netting with dodging *Panzerfaust* **[14]**. From this point can be seen the parallel road to the west along which the Fife and Forfars advanced. And to the east can be seen the line of telegraph poles disturbed by the Panther tank advancing from Estry.

If you are keen to explore the Nedforce position at les Grands Bonfaits **[15]**, it can be found **just 1.5km (0.9 miles)** east along this road, **towards Estry.** The position is unmarked, and the farmer has little knowledge of the events of August, 1944.

Back at the crossroad Calvary, descend south **into Presles [16]**, where you will get your first view of the Perrier Ridge ahead. Pass through Presles, and as you cross the broad valley, look left (east) along the dead ground along which the German infiltrators re-entered Presles. **After a climbing 'S' bend, stop** in a little lane to your right **[17]**. This is a good vantage point. To the north is Presles; west you can see Burcy church; and the road snaking diagonally up from Burcy to the Monmouths' and Fifes' headquarters box just over the hill at Forgues. Around you are the northern slopes of the Perrier Ridge, where 23/Hussars were deployed until the Germans back in Presles took them under fire.

A little further up the road, you will find the 11th Armoured Division memorial **[18].**

Resuming the route south, climb slowly through le Bas Perrier, le Haut Perrier, and finally **into Chênedollé** where the Tiger tank briefly halted the 23/Hussars **[19]**.

From Chênedollé, drive **west along the D303** (passing through some good examples of bocage sunken road!). Just 2km (1.2 miles) from Chênedollé, **stop at the road junction** where two small lanes form a 'V' to the right **[20]**. This is the point from which Steel Brownlie's four Shermans spearheaded the VIII Corps advance along the narrow track to the south. If you are feeling adventurous, pull on waterproofs and wellington boots and retrace Steel Brownlie's steps south along the path to the RUGBY Objective: the Vire-Vassy road.

Back at the junction, take the right hand road of the 'V', to the north east. You are following the assault of the *Frundsberg Panzergrenadiere* on 5 August. When you reach the top of the ridge, stop at a sharp left-hand bend. Here you will find twin monuments: to the 'Nor-Mons', and to Sidney Bates, VC **[21]**. This is as good a place as any to look down on the traffic on the RUGBY road and reflect on the significance of the penetration of the German line in Normandy: all the way from Caumont to this vital German artery.

The end of the tour. Twin monuments to the 'Nor-Mons' (left) and Sidney Bates, VC (right).

APPENDIX 1

WARTIME MAPS

Although sometimes criticised by soldiers, the maps produced by the British Army's Geographical Section were a major achievement. Without setting foot on French soil, this Section produced the first contoured maps of Normandy (pre-war French maps illustrated elevation using 'hachure').

Sometimes mistakes were made, and some of these have slipped into accounts of Operation BLUECOAT, confusing later authors and their readers as they confused soldiers in 1944. Usually, this came about when British map readers misunderstood the French tendency to position place names to the west of the village in question. So, Major Tollemache's account of his Coldstream Churchills being ambushed at la Morichèse actually refers to the sunken road at la Roque Poret. Similarly, units expecting to find St-Charles-de-Percy on the Vire road were puzzled to find the place a good mile to the east of the main highway (it had been confused with la Ferronnière). And British accounts of bitter fighting for Sourdeval are actually referring to the ridge line between Pavée and la Fauvellière.

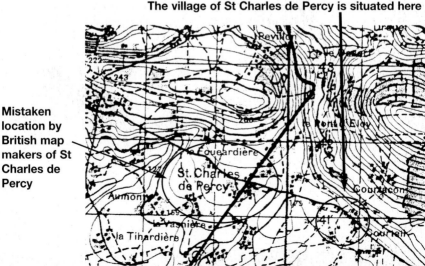

The village of St Charles de Percy is situated here

Mistaken location by British map makers of St Charles de Percy

APPENDIX 2

THE QUESTION OF VIRE

After nearly two months of bludgeoning by the British, the German front had held. Despite high rates of attrition, Army Group B showed no sign whatsoever of being about to shatter. Then on 1 August the British found themselves facing a gap in the defensive wall. The infantry divisions forming the left flank of *Panzergruppe West* and the Panzer division sent to buttress them all failed. Fortuitously, this occurred at a time and in a place where a dynamic corps commander was giving encouragement to the most creative and energetic divisional commander in the British sector, who in turn led the most effective British armoured division of the war.

The idea that Montgomery then missed a critical opportunity to shorten the war was proposed by Major J J How in 1981. Subsequent historians have debated his accusation. Without rehearsing all the arguments, it can safely be said that Montgomery did deny O'Connor and Roberts an opportunity which they realised was within their grasp. At a time when a small force could have seized Vire, Roberts recalled later:

'We had strict instructions from Monty that we were not – repeat NOT – to go into Vire. That was the American objective.'

One wonders what would have happened if a similar order had been given to American General George Patton, just short of a key strategic goal. Was Montgomery playing a political game? Was he in fact more stung by criticism of 'GOODWOOD' than he liked to make out? And was he seeking to restore his reputation by appeasing Eisenhower? There is another explanation.

By 1 August Operation BLUECOAT was turning into just the sort of fluid battle which Montgomery abhorred. Since 1944, Montgomery has been alternately lionized and reviled by historians. With time comes objectivity, and a general consensus is forming that the man was a competent general but perhaps not a great one. In Normandy, Montgomery was keen to avoid any encounter which he might lose. With this in mind, he was determined to not to let any battle run out of his control. Well aware of the shortcomings of the armies he commanded in 1944, he set his sights accordingly. His concern on 1 August was not pushing 11th Armoured Division still further 'into the blue', but rather getting some movement into XXX Corps' stalled offensive. Or as he would have put it, 'ungluing the battle' so that he could 'tidy it up'. Then he could restore a firm front line, bring up the rear elements, and then if the opportunity presented itself, have another 'big push'. On 2 August, he was more concerned with sacking Major General Bucknall (of XXX Corps), also Major General Erskine and Brigadier Hinde (of 7th Armoured), than with encouraging O'Connor to plunge into the unknown. By 3 August, Montgomery already had half a mind on the forthcoming Canadian assault to the east of Caen, Operation TOTALIZE.

With the benefit of hindsight, 'Pip' Roberts magnanimously conceded that the capture of Vire might have risked 11th Armoured Division becoming stranded beyond the reach of vital supplies and the range of VIII Corps' artillery. This is arguable. Perhaps it is most appropriate to end with Montgomery's own memoirs. His only comment on VIII Corps' operations on 2 August was that opposition to its advance 'was now becoming more stubborn', and that elements of the division reached the outskirts of Vire and patrols cut the Vire-Vassy road. He very much played down the role of BLUECOAT. This operation did not fit well into his vision of a campaign for Normandy which had gone strictly to plan – his plan.

Of the boundary issue, he chose to say not a word.

Reference

1 Blumenson, p 475.
2 Bennett, p 114-124.

INDEX

Allied Air Support, 14, 31-32, 123-124, 147, 154, 179
Allied Logistic Superiority, 15, 164-165, 176
Allied Vehicles & Weapons
Antiaircraft Tanks, 35-37, 166
6-Pounder Antitank Gun, 45, 47, 51-53, 95-97, 159-161
17-Pounder Antitank Gun, 15-16, 52, 107, 167
Bazooka, 114-115
25-Pounder Field Gun, 108, 120, 159, 164-165, 176-177
BESA, 40, 60-61
Bren Gun, 88, 159
Crab, 30, 34-36
Crocodile, 30, 37-39
Cromwell Tank, 61, 136-141, 154-159, 168
Churchill Tank, 31, 37, 39-54, 69
Dingo, 56-61
Firefly, 15-16, 145, 157, 161
PIAT, 65, 77, 115-118, 126-127
SABOT, 51-52, 95-96
Sexton, 165-167
Sherman Tank, 15-16, 111, 120-123, 145, 162
Staghound, 56-61
Stuart Tank, 113
Ammunition supply, 16, 176
Appliqué Armour, 49-50
Army Maps, 106-7, 181, 187

Bocage, 15, 24, 30, 70-71, 107
British Artillery Tactics, 14, 95-98, 111, 120, 159, 164-167, 176-177
British Units
21st Army Group, 103
2nd Army, 23, 28
VIII Corps, 25, 29-30, 62, 67, 99, 103, 169
XXX Corps, 23, 29, 42, 67, 99, 151, 169
Divisions
3rd, 146, 170-171
7th Armoured, 23-25, 151
11th Armoured, 25, 29, 55, 70-71, 145
15th (Scottish), 25, 29-30, 170
43rd, 23-24, 28, 47
50th, 23-24, 28
Guards Armoured, 25, 71-80, 102, 125, 144-145
Brigades
5th Guards (A) Bde, 73, 78
6th Guards (Tk) Bde, 25, 28,

29, 68
29th Bde, 151, 168
31st (Tk) Bde, 29
32nd Guards Bde, 73
44 Bde, 170,
46 Bde, 46
159 Bde, 151
185 Bde, 146, 168, 171
227 Bde, 30, 41
Regiments
21/Antitank, 167
75/Antitank, 100, 107
2/A&SH, 25, 41-42, 47-54
Ayrshire Yeomanry, 108, 120, 159, 164-165, 176
9/Cameronian, 30-40, 95
4/(Tk) Coldstream Guards, 41-42, 95
5/Coldstream Guards, 73-76, 142-145
5/DCLI, 92-93
2/Fife & Forfarshire Yeomanry, 55, 101, 107, 118-125, 153-154
2/Gordon Highlanders, 30-46
1/(Motor) Grenadier Guards, 76-77, 141-142
2/(A) Grenadier Guards, 76-77, 141-142
4/(Tk) Grenadier Guards, 30-40
10/HLI, 41-46
2/Household Cavalry, 56-61, 80-81, 100
23/Hussars, 56, 62-66, 80, 101, 106, 109-118, 173
Inns of Court, 100, 137
2/(A) Irish Guards, 73-76, 142
3/Irish Guards, 143-144
6/KOSB, 26, 98-99, 170
2/KSLI, 171
4/KSLI, 55, 84-86, 100, 125-128, 159-162
Leicestershire Yeomanry, 166-167
Lothian & Border Yeomanry, 35-36
3/Monmouthshire, 56, 64-66, 101, 107, 118-125
2/Northamptonshire Yeomanry, 61, 101, 105-106, 154-159, 168
2/Oxf & Bucks, 19
15/Reconnaissance, 95
141 RAC ('The Buffs'), 37-39
8/RB, 55, 83-84, 100-101, 107, 109-118, 142
8/Royal Scots, 170
6/Royal Scots Fus, 98, 170

13/RHA, 108, 165-166, 176
3/RTR, 55, 83-84, 100, 125-126, 159-162
3 (Tk) Scots Guards, 41-42, 47-54
7/Seaforth, 46
2/Warwickshire, 171-172
2/(A) Welsh Guards, 136-141, 144
Battlegroups
Nedforce, 125-128, 159-163
Nor-Mons, 174-178
Steel, 123-125, 153-154

Casualties: American, 17
British, 14
Co-operation Infantry and Tanks, 29-32, 68-77, 134

Demolition of Tanks, 83

Friendly Fire, 19-20, 123-124, 175-176

German Armour Superiority, 111, 154, 157, 162, 168
German Battle Tactics, 86-89, 112, 162-164
German Infiltration Tactics, 167-168
German Units
7th Army, 67, 129
Panzergruppe West, 67, 103, 129
II SS-Panzer Korps, 13-14, 103-105, 113-114
II Fallschirmjäger Korps, 61-
LXXIV Korps, 29, 61, 67, 86
Divisions
3 Fallschirmjäger, 61-62, 129, 149, 157
9 SS-Panzerdivision 'Hohenstaufen', 104-105, 125, 128-134, 142, 169, 171-172
10 SS-Panzerdivision 'Frundsberg', 104, 172-178
12 SS-Panzerdivision 'Hitler Jugend', 13, 90-91, 104
21 Panzerdivision, 23, 56-61, 65-66, 74-81, 89-99, 103, 129
116 Panzerdivision, 122
Panzer-Lehr, 18-20
276. Infanterie, 23
326. Infanterie, 25, 28, 40, 61, 86-89
752. Infanterie, 40

Battalions
9. SS-Pz.Aufkl.Abt., 109, 144-145, 148-150
125. Panzergrenadier Rgt., 99
326. Fusilierbataillon, 86
schwere Panzerabteilung 503, 128-133
schwere SS-Panzerabteilung 102, 117-118
schwere Panzerjaeger Abteilung 654, 48-54
Kampfgruppen
KG Fröhlich, 138-143
KG Meyer, 129, 144-145, 153
AG Olboeter, 152-153, 169
KG Weiss, 130-133, 146-159, 172

German Vehicles & Weapons
7.5 cm PaK40, 50
8.8 cm Gun, 45, 48-51
Half-tracks, 109, 118, 125, 128-129, 150, 154
Jagdpanther, 48-54, 86
Machine Guns, 86-89, 136
Nebelwerfer, 93-4, 173, 176
Panzer IV, 18, 77-83, 91-92, 94, 177
Panzer V (Panther), 18, 111, 161-162
Panzer VI (Tiger/King Tiger), 92-99, 154-158, 173
Panzerfaust, 24, 68, 110
Panzerschreck, 68, 115-116
Sturmgeschütz, 133-136
Wespe, 152

Mines, 32-35, 65, 120
Motor Transport, 76

Operations
COBRA, 15-20
EPSOM, 13, 25-26
DREADNOUGHT, 21
GOODWOOD, 14-15, 22-26, 145
Lüttich, 178-180
SPRING, 15
TOTALIZE, 169, 180

People
Allies
Adair, Major General Allan, 26
Bates VC, Corporal Sidney, 177
Bradley, General Omar, 21
Brownlie, Lieutenant W Steel, 118-125, 153
Bucknall, Lt. General, 23, 151, 188

Eisenhower, Dwight D., 14-15, 22
Dempsey, Lt Gen Miles, 21, 26
Farrell, Captain Charles, 52-54
Gerow, General L., 61
Kenneth, Major John, 41, 48
Leigh-Mallory, Air Chief Marshall Sir Trafford, 19
Lomas, Cpl Ron, 25, 26-27, 52-53
MacMillan, Major General G., 30, 42-44
Marshall-Cornwall, Lt. James, 39
Montgomery, Field Marshall Bernard Law, 9-14, 22-23, 105, 149, 164, 188
O'Connor, General Sir Richard, 25, 72-73
Patton, Lt General George, 9, 13, 89-90
Powle, Lieutenant 'Dickie', 56-61
Roberts, Major General 'Pip', 9-13, 26, 28, 62, 99-102, 105, 145
Tedder, Air Chief Marshall Sir Arthur, 22
Thornburn, Major 'Ned', 124-128
Verney, Brigadier, 42-44, 46
Whitelaw, Captain William, 52
Germans
Bittrich, SS-Obergruppenführer Wilhelm, 104, 178
Dollmann, Generaloberst Friedrich, 105
Drabich-Waechter, Generalleutnant Viktor, 86, 89
Eberbach, General Heinrich, 103, 171-172, 178
Gräbner, SS-Hauptsturmführer Viktor, 109, 148-150
Guderian, General Heinz, 163
Feuchtinger, Generalmajor Edgar, 89, 91, 93, 99
Harmel, SS-Standartenführer Heinz, 177-178
Hausser, SS-Oberstgruppenführer Paul, 67
Hitler, Adolph: 23, 152, 178-179
Kluge, Generalfeldmarschall Günther Hans, 67-68, 151-153, 169, 172-173, 179-180
Meindl, General Eugen, 61-62, 150
Meyer, SS-Oberstumbannführer Otto, 129, 143
Scheiber, Leutnant 49-54
Straube, General Erich, 46, 71, 89
Weiss, Sturmbannführer Hans, 130-133

Wittmann, SS-Obersturmführer Michael, 131
Places
Burcy, 120-121, 144, 168, 175
Caen, 9, 15, 23
Caumont, 30, 32-37, 68, 103
Chênedollé, 114-118, 146-147, 169, 172
Forêt l'Evêque, 58-68
Hill 226, 29, 47-54
Hill 238, 74-76
Hill 309, 29, 44-46, 93-99
la Bistière, 155-159, 168, 171
la Ferrière-Harang, 58-63
la Ferronnière, 79, 139, 143, 187
le Bény-Bocage, 66, 80-85, 150
le Tourneur, 77-78
les Loges, 47-54
les Grands Bonfaits, 126-128, 141, 151, 159-162
Lutain Wood, 32-41
Montchauvet, 133-135, 138, 142, 170-171
Montchamp, 135-136, 138-142
'Mortar Gulch', 79, 85, 138, 143, 170-171
Perrier Ridge, 120-121, 151, 168, 172-178
Presles, 111-113
St-Charles-de-Percy, 138-140, 142, 187
St-Martin-des-Besaces, 55-58, 72, 103, 166
Sept Vents, 30-37, 41-42
Souleuvre River, 57-60, 65-66, 72, 78, 101-1-2, 107, 140
The 'Suisse Normande', 106-107
Villers-Bocage, 131
Vire, 105-106, 144-150, 152-155, 180, 187-188

Reconnaissance, 56-61, 77-81, 100-101, 109, 113, 136-141, 150

ULTRA, 23, 169, 179

United States Units
First US Army Group, 23
V Corps, 61-62
XIX Corps, 62
First Army, 23
2nd Division, 62
5th Division, 26, 61-62

Wireless Communications, 41, 59-60, 126, 161-162